TOWARDS
A PAPACY
IN
COMMUNION

UT UNUM SINT: STUDIES ON PAPAL PRIMACY

TOWARDS A PAPACY IN COMMUNION

PERSPECTIVES FROM VATICAN COUNCILS I AND II

HERMANN J. POTTMEYER

TRANSLATED BY MATTHEW J. O'CONNELL

A Herder and Herder Book
The Crossroad Publishing Company
New York

The Crossroad Publishing Company
16 Penn Plaza – 481 Eighth Avenue, Suite 1550
New York, NY 10001

Printed in the United States of America

Library of Congress Cataloging-in-Publication Data
Pottmeyer, Hermann Josef.
    Towards a papacy in communion : perspectives from Vatican Councils
  I & II / Hermann J. Pottmeyer ; translated by Matthew J. O'Connell.
      p. cm.
    Includes bibliographical references (p.).
    ISBN 0-8245-1776-8 (pbk.)
    1. Popes – Primacy – History of doctrines – 19th century. 2. Popes –
  Primacy – History of doctrines – 20th century. 3. Vatican Council
  (1st : 1869–1870) 4. Vatican Council (2nd : 1962–1965) 5. Papacy
  and Christian union. 6. Petrine office. I. Title.
  BX1805.P67 1998
  262'.13 – dc21   98-24303

Contents

Preface

Nine years as a student in Rome (1955–64) gave me the opportunity to observe three popes up close: Pius XII, John XXIII, and Paul VI. Each of them exercised his office in his own unique manner. I also witnessed the first two sessions of the Second Vatican Council. My experiences in those years, and my study of church history, made me aware of how differently the Petrine office can be exercised. The council brought home to me the church's character as a worldwide fellowship and its capacity for self-renewal.

Those who live for a time in Rome experience the church's age, but also its youth. They experience the church's breadth and diversity, its religious and human wealth, but also the limits and weaknesses of its representatives and members. Since the council I have been able, as a visiting professor and a member of various Vatican commissions, to observe postconciliar developments at the church's center.

The fathers and theologians of Vatican II were convinced that the Petrine office was a gift of God to his church. At the same time, the council's overwhelming majority was clearly determined to put an end to the Vatican centralization which had developed since Vatican I. In this they were motivated primarily by theological and not merely by practical considerations. They understood the universal church as a community of local churches, requiring collegial leadership open to participation by all.

Increasing criticism of church centralization since the council shows that the desire of the council's majority has not been fulfilled. Those responsible for this centralization continue to appeal to the dogmas of Vatican I. All attempts to maintain total control from the center show, however, that in a church which is now truly worldwide such centralization exceeds the abilities of even the most skilled administrators. Moreover, Vatican centralization encounters a further obstacle: the church's growing awareness that it is a community of churches — a conception firmly rooted in the documents of Vatican II.

The pages that follow are intended to show that there is no firm theological foundation for Vatican I's centralization and thus to open a way out of the dead-end street into which centralization has led us. The proposals outlined here are based on the documents of Vatican II, along with a careful analysis of papal jurisdiction and infallibility in the dynamics of Vatican I. These proposals are intended as an aid in a true understanding of the Petrine office as a ministry of communion within the universal church — an understanding which will enable all Christians to recognize the office of Peter's successor as God's gift to his church. Pope John Paul's invitation, in his encyclical *Ut unum sint,* to a dialogue about his office is the book's point of departure.

During more than a decade a number of colleagues and friends deserve my thanks: Michael J. Buckley, Avery Dulles, Michael J. Himes, John Jay Hughes, Robert A. Krieg, Matthew Lamb, Fred Lawrence, Leo O'Donovan, and Thomas F. O'Meara. They have brought me into closer contact with theological study and teaching in the United States. I am also grateful to colleagues who have especially enriched my ecclesiological thinking: Patrick Granfield, Joseph A. Komonchak, Richard P. McBrien, Ladislas Örsy, and Francis A. Sullivan.

My special thanks to the admirable Cardinal Joseph Bernardin, the late archbishop of Chicago, who hosted me in his residence and shared with me his thoughtful reflections on the reform of church and papacy.

It was a valuable experience to spend a term as Visiting Professor in South Bend, and I am especially grateful to colleagues at Notre Dame for the dialogue and friendship provided there. I am grateful, too, for the hospitality extended to me when I have been invited to speak at other U.S. institutions: Catholic University of America, which awarded me the Johannes Quasten Medal; Boston College; Fordham University; and Georgetown University.

I have learned much about the interplay between communication theory and theology from Professor Frances Forde Plude; her knowledge, enthusiasm, and friendship have provided encouragement and practical assistance to me in many ways as this book was written.

Finally, I thank my research assistants, Christian Heller and Tobias Specker, and my secretary, Ursula Bickel, for their enthusiastic help. Special gratitude goes to Matthew O'Connell, who performed the difficult task of translating the text.

Abbreviations

DS   *Enchiridion Symbolorum, Definitionum et Declara-
      tionum de Rebus Fidei et Morum,* ed. H. Denzinger, rev.
      A. Schönmetzer, 36th ed. (Freiburg: Herder, 1976).

GS   *Gaudium et spes,* Pastoral Constitution on the Church in
      the Modern World, Second Vatican Council.

LG   *Lumen gentium,* Dogmatic Constitution on the Church,
      Second Vatican Council.

M   *Sacrorum Conciliorum nova et amplissima Collectio,*
      vols. 1–53, ed. G. D. Mansi and others (1759–1927).

ND   *The Christian Faith in the Doctrinal Documents of the
      Catholic Church,* ed. J. Neuner and J. Dupuis, 6th ed.
      (New York: Alba House, 1996).

UUS   *Ut unum sint,* Encyclical Letter on Commitment to
      Ecumenism, John Paul II (Vatican City: Libreria Editrice
      Vaticana, 1995).

CHAPTER ONE

The Challenge to a New Dialogue on the Papacy

The Challenge from the Ecumenical Situation

May 25, 1995, the day on which Pope John Paul II published his encyclical letter *Ut unum sint* "on Commitment to Ecumenism," may one day be remembered as having inaugurated a new era in the history of Christianity. The reason: this encyclical could begin a development in the course of which the papacy in its Latin form might become an ecumenical Petrine ministry.

Such a hope is well founded. The encyclical correctly says that "after centuries of bitter controversies, the other Churches and Ecclesial Communities are more and more taking a fresh look at this ministry of unity" (UUS 89). As far as his own office is concerned, the pope is aware that "what should have been a service sometimes manifested itself in a very different light" (UUS 95). He therefore asks other Christians for forgiveness and admits his own special responsibility for the unity of Christians. The tone is a very personal one when he writes:

> I am convinced that I have a particular responsibility in this regard, above all in acknowledging the ecumenical aspirations of the majority of the Christian Communities and in heeding the request made of me to find a way of exercising the primacy which, while in no way renouncing what is essential to its mission, is nonetheless open to a new situation. (UUS 95)

Pope John Paul II's admission of the possibility that the present way of exercising the primacy is no longer in keeping with today's ecumenical situation has caused many Christians to sit up and take notice. For by this admission he opens the way for an ecumenical Petrine ministry. The pope then draws the logical conclusion that this task cannot be successfully carried out by the pope and the Roman Catholic Church alone. A Petrine ministry that is recognized by all Christians can take form only within an ecumenical dialogue.

This accounts for the pope's moving invitation to all Christians, the new tone of which is unmistakable:

> This is an immense task, which we cannot refuse and which I cannot carry out by myself. Could not the real but imperfect communion existing between us persuade Church leaders and their theologians to engage with me in a patient and fraternal dialogue on this subject, a dialogue in which, leaving useless controversies behind, we could listen to one another, keeping before us only the will of Christ for his Church and allowing ourselves to be deeply moved by his plea "that they may all be one... so that the world may believe that you have sent me" (Jn 17:21)? (UUS 96)

It is noteworthy that the invitation to converse with him about the reform of his office is directed by the pope first of all to non-Catholic church leaders and theologians, and not to the bishops and theologians of his own church. The fact is remarkable for two reasons. On the one hand, the desire for the reform of the papacy in the non-Catholic world is undoubtedly more wide-ranging than that in the Catholic Church. The pope is thus opening himself to a greater challenge. On the other hand, the pope's readiness for reform has caused surprise within the Catholic Church. For here people have been complaining that the beginnings of a reform after Vatican II have been halted during the last two decades and that a growing centralization along the lines of Vatican I has been observable. For this reason, there have been doubts in the Catholic Church about the Vatican's readiness for reform.

In recent times the Vatican has paid little attention to the reform proposals of Catholic bishops and theologians. Anyway, the pope does not exclude the bishops and theologians of his own church from the dialogue. In his address to Ecumenical Patriarch Demetrios I, which he cites, he says: "I insistently pray the

Holy Spirit to shine his light upon us, enlightening all the Pastors and theologians of our Churches, that we may seek — together, of course — the forms in which this ministry may accomplish a service of love recognized by all concerned" (UUS 95).

But, with their eyes on recent developments within the Roman Catholic Church, non-Catholics also have expressed doubts about the Vatican's readiness for reform. Some of the Vatican's interventions in the ecumenical dialogue seem to justify these doubts. Finally, the encyclical itself provides the occasion for critical questions. Some critics find that the encyclical "insists on an unrestricted claim to primacy in accordance with the papal dogmas of Vatican I,"[1] and it refers, in fact, explicitly to that council (UUS 94). The appeal to Vatican I contrasts strongly with the effort of the encyclical to emphasize the service aspect of the papal office and to insist that the primacy is to be exercised only jointly with the college of bishops. The tension is the same as that found in the documents of Vatican II between the understanding of the church as people of God and as community of particular churches, and the unqualified repetition of the formulas of Vatican I, which give a centralized picture of the church.

Despite these doubts, it would be a disastrous mistake not to take the pope at his word. His invitation is a sign of the extent to which the separated Christians and churches have already drawn closer to each other. Furthermore, the question of the papal office can no longer be left out of consideration within the ecumenical dialogue or discussed only in passing. Admittedly, from a theological point of view this question as such is neither fundamental nor central. On the other hand, many other and more fundamental theological questions are bound up with it. Therefore the extent of ecumenical consensus on more central questions will be demonstrated by agreement on an ecumenical Petrine ministry.

But the question of the Petrine office is far more than simply a theological measure of ecumenical agreement achieved. Discussion of it is burdened by the handicap of historical experiences

---

1. Heinrich Leipold, "Papstamt und Petrusdienst aus evangelischer Sicht," *Una Sancta* 5 (1992): 158.

arising from the misuse of this office and from exaggerated claims to papal power. But since the lack of a universal ministry of unity outside the Catholic Church has also led to experiences that have become a burden, there is a rising hope today in the ecumenical movement that an ecumenical Petrine ministry, exercised in accordance with the gospel, may be a special gift God has for Christianity.

Whether this hope is a solid one or whether the office of pope will continue to be seen by many as the greatest obstacle on the way of ecumenism, as Paul VI said of it in 1967,[2] will therefore be shown first of all by whether the Catholic Church itself achieves such a reform of this office. Many of the fathers and theologians of Vatican II intended such a reform, seeking therein to renew the common tradition of the East and the West during the first millennium. According to prevailing opinion both outside and inside the Catholic Church, the interpretation of that tradition and the exercise of the papal office are still largely dependent on Vatican I. But, as the expression of a will to papal centralization, the formulation of the primacy of jurisdiction and the papal magisterium by Vatican I is undoubtedly unacceptable to non-Catholic Christians.

At Vatican II it was in fact precisely these dogmatic formulations of Vatican I that limited the development of a *communio* ecclesiology as understood in the tradition of the early church. These dogmas have also limited and hindered reform in the postconciliar development of the Catholic Church, and they show their effects even in the surprisingly open encyclical *Ut unum sint*. The observation of this fact strengthens the impression, even in sectors of the ecumenical movement, that the greatest hindrance to an ecumenical agreement is not the papal office as such, but rather the way in which Vatican I formulated the Petrine ministry. A Protestant theologian like Peter Brunner, who originated the sharp remark that Vatican I "slammed the door shut,"[3] is able to imagine an ecclesial structure compatible with the scriptures in

---

2. *Acta apostolicae sedis* 59 (1967): 498.
3. Peter Brunner, *Bemühungen um die einigende Wahrheit: Aufsätze* (Göttingen: Vandenhoeck & Ruprecht, 1977), 32.

which "many pastors and bishops are gathered around a *single pastor and bishop.*"[4]

For these reasons, the Catholic Church must answer the following questions: Does it see the formulations of Vatican I as the only possible and most complete expression of its belief in a divinely willed Petrine office, or is a formulation of this ministry conceivable that takes into account the *communio* tradition of the first millennium and the new ecumenical situation? Or, in relation to the exercise of papal primacy: Is the centralized exercise of the primacy, as it has prevailed since the nineteenth century, the only possible form that does justice to the formulations of Vatican I, or are the formulations of Vatican I open to a more effective practice of *communio?*

Or, finally, to use the language of the encyclical *Ut unum sint:* Do the formulations of Vatican I permit us "to find a way of exercising the primacy which, while in no way renouncing what is essential to its mission, is nonetheless open to a new situation" (UUS 95) and open also to the tradition of the undivided church? In fact, the encyclical cites that tradition: "For a whole millennium Christians were united in 'a brotherly fraternal communion of faith and sacramental life.... If disagreements in belief and discipline arose among them, the Roman See acted by common consent as moderator' " (UUS 95). Here the encyclical speaks not, in the language of Vatican I, of a "prince," but of a "moderator."

The Challenge from the Globalization of the Catholic Church

The ecumenical movement undoubtedly represents the most important demand of the Catholic Church that it ask itself these questions. But there are also good reasons for these questions considering the changes within the Catholic Church itself. In the twentieth century the social form of the Catholic Church has

---

4. Peter Brunner, "Evangelium und Papsttum," *Evangelisch-lutherische Kirchenzeitung* 10 (1956): 442.

greatly changed: It has become a global church. The dogmas of Vatican I, on the other hand, are still shaped primarily by the European situation of the eighteenth and nineteenth centuries. Today the Catholic Church is increasingly losing its Eurocentric character. That was already clear at Vatican II, which therefore expressly gave thought to the task of a new inculturation and to diversity as a mark of Catholicity.

With the globalization of the Catholic Church and with its increasing cultural differentiation, it is also becoming increasingly difficult to understand and exercise papal primacy as a central administrative authority. Such an exercise leads to increasing conflicts with particular and regional churches or to anti-Vatican sentiments within them. Even the Roman Curia must feel overtaxed by such a task. The Vatican reacted to this situation by internationalizing the Roman Curia and the college of cardinals, as well as by instituting regular synods of bishops and by convoking synods of regional churches, held in Rome. All these measures can have their value, but they also reflect the fact that the Vatican is holding fast to a centralizing conception of papal primacy, one which it regards as made obligatory by Vatican I.

The recently increasing centralization criticized by Catholic bishops and theologians is due to the Vatican's concern that the new variety of mentalities in the church represents not only an enrichment but can also become a force that will destroy ecclesial unity. But the Vatican's centralizing reaction does not respect the structure of the universal church as a community of churches; this *communio* nature of the church is exactly what Vatican II sought to strengthen.

Indeed, the Vatican centralization is proving ever more unsuitable for doing justice to the new situation even within the Catholic Church. It was this realization, not anti-Vatican sentiment, that motivated many fathers of Vatican Council II in their wish for the development of a *communio* form and *communio* praxis of papal primacy that would correspond to the *communio* nature of the church. But, according to other council fathers, such a development was opposed by the binding force of Vatican I. It is therefore not only the new ecumenical situation but also, and no less, the changes in the Catholic Church itself that are necessitating a critical reexamination of Vatican I.

In light of all that has been said, we can distinguish two goals for a new dialogue about the Petrine office. The first goal, which is to be sought first, is an intra-Catholic reform of the papal office corresponding to the essential structure of the church as a community of churches as well as to the new situation of greater Catholic variety. The attainment of this goal is the first and indispensable step on the way to an ecumenical Petrine ministry, the creation of which is the more important goal and the greater challenge. As far as the attainment of the first goal is concerned, there are two tasks: first, a critical consideration of whether the dogmatic formulations of Vatican I necessarily block the reform of the papal office, and, second, a logical continuation of the reform of the church envisaged by Vatican II.

Misunderstandings That Hinder the New Dialogue

Anyone taking up the task of critically examining the dogmas of Vatican I must plan on meeting two misunderstandings, which must be addressed at the outset. They are misunderstandings that, to a large extent, dominate the discussion and are a greater obstacle to a new dialogue on the papacy than even the dogmas of Vatican I.

The first misunderstanding consists in thinking that a reform of the papacy is possible only if one relativizes or even denies the binding character of the two dogmas of Vatican I on the primacy of jurisdiction and on the infallibility of the pope. This view is maintained both by defenders of the irreformability of these dogmas and of the centralizing form of the papacy, and by many critics of Vatican I. But a relativization or denial of the truth of these dogmas is not required for reform. We can be convinced that Vatican I formulated and defined the authority of the Petrine office in a true and valid way, and yet be conscious of the contextual character and reference of the definition. That is, we can regard these dogmas as a possible and legitimate definition of the

Petrine office and authority, without therefore having to consider them the *only* possible formulation and definition. This is true even though the majority of the council fathers in their situation regarded this definition as the only adequate one and even though the council condemned certain conceptions of Petrine authority. The condemned conceptions may in fact no longer be held. But at that time many of the council fathers were thoroughly aware that the Petrine office had been differently formulated and exercised at other periods, and that those forms and formulations were likewise part of Catholic tradition.

Today, then, the only dispute can be about whether the definition of Vatican I represents the only possible formulation of the Petrine office and whether the resultant centralizing exercise of its authority is the only adequate form of its exercise. Even though he did not intend to decide this dispute, Pope John Paul II made a clear reference to it. In his encyclical *Ut unum sint* he makes a distinction between the "way of exercising the primacy which . . . is open to a new situation" and "what is essential to its mission" (UUS 95). In saying this, the pope is picking up a statement of Vatican II: "For the deposit of faith or revealed truths are one thing; the manner in which they are formulated, without violence to their meaning and significance, is another" (GS 62).

Without thereby calling into question the truth of the definition of Vatican I, the claim may very well be made that the church and its magisterium can formulate the authority of the Petrine office in a different way that corresponds better to the nature of the church and to the new situation. The Congregation for the Doctrine of the Faith made a comment along these lines in 1973: "It sometimes happens that some dogmatic truth is first expressed incompletely (but not falsely), and at a later date, when considered in a broader context of faith or human knowledge, it receives a fuller and more perfect expression."[5] The same congregation called attention to the contextual nature of many dogmatic formulations (which certainly applies to the definition of Vati-

---

5. Congregation for the Doctrine of the Faith, Declaration in Defence of the Catholic Doctrine on the Church against Certain Errors of the Present Day, *Mysterium Ecclesiae* (Vatican City: Libreria Editrice Vaticana, 1973), 12.

can I): "Even though the truths which the church intends to teach through her dogmatic formulas are distinct from the changeable conceptions of a given epoch and can be expressed without them, nevertheless it can sometimes happen that these truths may be enunciated by the sacred magisterium in terms that bear traces of such conceptions."[6]

It is, therefore, a misunderstanding of the binding force of Vatican I to claim that its definition must, no matter what, be regarded as the only possible and the best formulation of the authority of the Petrine office.

The second misunderstanding is likewise widespread. It is the view that the reduction of Vatican centralization means a weakening of the authority of the Petrine office by strengthening collegial cooperation in the government of the universal church. Consequently, some individuals speak of a weakening of papal primacy in order to make room for collegiality; others reject a strengthening of collegiality because, in their view, it means a weakening of the primacy and is opposed to Vatican I. This misunderstanding is based on the idea that papal primacy is something like an all-embracing power of a kind that is limited, as from outside, by the power of the bishops or by the rights of the particular churches to play a collaborative role.

Behind this idea is the modern concept of all-embracing sovereign power that developed in the European states of the eighteenth and nineteenth centuries. In the nineteenth century this concept was also frequently applied to the supreme power in the church and did indeed play a part in the conception of papal primacy. In the logic of this conception, every sharing by the bishops in the government of the universal church appears to be in fact a limitation on the papal primacy.

This conception, however, is not part of the Catholic tradition nor was it accepted by Vatican I and II. Both councils no doubt placed the emphasis at times on the pope's freedom to act at any time without the formal cooperation of the bishops. That emphasis fostered the misunderstanding in question. But, after speaking

---

6. Ibid., 13.

of the special duties and rights of the pope, the encyclical *Ut unum sint* says, with obvious reference to that misunderstanding:

> All this however must always be done in communion. When the Catholic Church affirms that the office of the Bishop of Rome corresponds to the will of Christ, she does not separate this office from the mission entrusted to the whole body of bishops, who are also "vicars and ambassadors of Christ." The Bishop of Rome is a member of the "College," and the Bishops are his brothers in the ministry. (UUS 95)

It is therefore a misunderstanding to think that the logical development of collegial cooperation and of the communal structure means a minimizing or weakening of the God-given authority of the Petrine office, or that this development could be accomplished only in that way. From the viewpoint of theology, the authority of the pope and the authority of the bishops are not competing powers, but strengthen each other in the spirit of a shared collegial responsibility. For this reason, Vatican I cites Pope Gregory I: "My honor is the honor of the whole Church. My honor is the firm strength of my brothers. I am truly honored when due honor is paid to each and every one" (ND 827). In a theological perspective, then, the reduction of papal centralization does not mean a weakening of the Petrine office but a strengthening of it, because its honor is increased by promoting collegiality and participation.[7]

---

7. See Patrick Granfield, *The Papacy in Transition* (New York: Doubleday, 1980).

CHAPTER TWO

From Witness to Monarch: Development of, or Change in, Papal Primacy?

After the discussion of the misunderstandings that often hinder an unprejudiced evaluation of Vatican I, we can now turn to the first task of the two mentioned. Our intention here is to answer the question: Is the centralizing form which the papacy has had since the last century the necessary result of Vatican I, or does this form owe more to the historical situation in the nineteenth century? We need to outline, in the second chapter, the historical development and then, in the third chapter, the historical situation in the nineteenth century.[1]

The "Development" of Papal Primacy

It has been customary, down to the present time, to speak of a consistent development of papal primacy. This development is thought of either as a logical explication of what is inherently implicit in the original reality or as an organic unfolding of the full form from the original bud. Continuity and progress,

---

1. See Hans von Campenhausen, *Ecclesiastical Authority and Spiritual Power in the Church of the First Three Centuries* (London: Black, 1969); Yves Congar, *A History of Theology* (New York: Doubleday, 1968); Yves Congar, *L'Église de Saint Augustin à l'époque moderne* (Paris: Cerf, 1970); Klaus Schatz, *Papal Primacy from Its Origins to the Present* (Collegeville, Minn.: Liturgical Press, 1996).

it is said, characterize this development. From this point of view, earlier forms of papal primacy were only defective transitional forms, until its full truth and perfect form were reached at Vatican I.

This idea of an unbroken logical or organic development is questionable both historically and theologically. In the realm of history it ignores the fact that along with an undeniable continuity, breaks with venerable structural traditions occurred. In addition, different metaphors and motifs, models and influences alternated, without any logical or organic continuity to be found among them. The idea is also theologically questionable, because it sees the forms taken by the Petrine office in earlier ages as having been defective. Is the understanding of the Petrine ministry which the fathers of the church or the bishops and popes of earlier centuries had to be judged faulty because it did not completely correspond to that of Vatican I?

It is more correct, both theologically and historically, to speak of a plurality of possible and actual embodiments of the Petrine office. Each of these embodiments is to be judged by whether it served the welfare and mission of the church in a given age and was consistent with the commission given to Peter. Vatican I cannot be the ultimate standard for all the ages.

As a matter of fact, during the lengthy series of diverse embodiments of the Petrine office a kind of change did take place. But this change is not to be understood as simply a progressive development of the commission given to Peter in the Bible. Instead, the change in the form of the Petrine office arose out of the church's developing awareness of itself. It was in the context of this formation of a self-consciousness that the role of the pope in the church also changed from witness to monarch.

We may speak of two paradigms of ecclesial self-consciousness, although this reduction to two is something of an oversimplification. The first paradigm was characteristic of the first millennium, the second of the second millennium. Each of the paradigms was matched by a specific conception and embodiment of the Petrine office.

The Paradigm of Church of the First Millennium: Witness of Tradition

From the outset the church knew that it was duty bound to preserve the apostolic tradition and hand it on unadulterated. All
the institutions that developed in the church — sacred scripture,
professions of faith, the liturgy, the ministries — were to assist
in meeting this responsibility. The main concern of the church of
the first millennium was to avoid changing anything in its tradition. Consequently, everything new that arose was traced back to
the age of the apostles. If doubts arose about what belonged to
the apostolic tradition, the answer was sought in the tradition of
the churches that had been founded by the apostles and, later on,
in the consensus of all the churches. The most important mark
of the church was its apostolicity. The paradigm of the church
of the first millennium may best be described in this way: The
church understood itself to be witness to the apostolic tradition.[2]

This was true also of the Roman church and its bishop. The
church of Rome enjoyed special regard because, along with the
tombs of the Apostles Peter and Paul, it also preserved their tradition. Other churches, too, took their lead from the church of
Rome. Consequently, as the local churches grew together into the
universal church, Rome became the most important center of the
ecclesial community. And as the bishops emerged as the leaders
and representatives of their local churches, the special standing of
the Roman church left its imprint on the authority of the Roman
bishop. He was regarded as witness to, and protector of, the tradition of the Apostles Peter and Paul, which possessed a special
authority for the entire church.

One element in the safeguarding of the church's apostolicity
was that the bishops traced their office back to the apostles. They
understood themselves to be the successors of the apostles and
the heirs of the apostolic commission. In the third century the
bishops of Rome began to appeal to Peter and his commission-

---

2. See Hermann-Josef Sieben, *Die Konzilsidee der Alten Kirche* (Paderborn:
Schöningh, 1979).

ing by Jesus as the justification of their own special authority. Increasingly, it was no longer simply the special standing of the tradition of the Roman church that grounded the special author- ity of the Roman bishop, but his special mission as successor of Peter. This shift became clear when Pope Leo I, in the fifth cen- tury, described himself no longer as simply "successor of Peter" but as "representative of Peter." He acted now in the place of Peter whenever the preservation of the tradition called for an active intervention.

The special authority of the Roman bishop and his increas- ingly active role were strengthened by the fact that the political model provided by ancient Rome began to influence the self- understanding of the Roman bishop: the model, that is, of Rome as "capital of the world" and of the Roman emperor as a law- giver who was vested with the "plenitude of power." The papacy made its own the heritage of ancient Rome and of the Roman emperor.

It must be emphasized, however, that throughout the entire first millennium the popes understood themselves to be, first and foremost, witnesses to the apostolic and universal tradition of the church. Their universal pastoral function consisted in preserving this tradition and in restoring the inherited order of the church when it was violated. As tradition was conceived at that period, it included not only the profession of faith but also the discipline and organization of the church. Since the authority of the episco- pal office was also part of the church's organization, the pope was bound to respect and protect the authority of his fellow bishops and their share of responsibility for the entire church.

In fact the collegiality of the bishops was a constitutive element in a church that took as its supreme principle the immutability of the apostolic tradition. As the apostolic circle was made up of Peter and his fellow apostles, so the college of bishops was made up of the pope and his fellow bishops. Collegiality was an ele- ment in the apostolicity of the church and, no less, an expression of the church's structure as a community of churches.[3] But it was

---

3. See Wilhelm De Vries, *Orient et Occident: Les structures ecclésiales vues*

also an element of a church whose most important task was to be witness to tradition. The greater the number of witnesses in agreement, the more authoritative the testimony. A single witness, no matter how superior his jurisdictional authority, is less authoritative than many witnesses. This was the basis of the commonly held conviction that in matters of faith a council or the unanimous testimony of the episcopate enjoys greater authority than the testimony of the pope alone. Until Vatican I and its dogma of papal infallibility this conviction was the main objection against a monarchical conception of the primacy.

On the Way to a New Paradigm of Church and to Monarchical Primacy

The new millennium brought with it a change of paradigms in the self-understanding of the church. The concern to preserve the apostolic tradition did, of course, remain obligatory for the church of the second millennium, but the church as community of witnesses became increasingly a papal monarchy, with the pope fashioning the church by defining its tradition and organizing its social life by legislation. That change means a shift from the paradigm of the church that understood itself exclusively as witness of apostolic tradition to the paradigm of a church which became aware that the preservation of tradition called for action to redefine the tradition as the circumstances may require. Thus the church discovered itself as an active subject shaping itself, its tradition, and its life. Within this process the papacy was of special importance. On the one hand the new role of the pope became possible only within the new self-understanding of the church; on the other hand it was the growing jurisdictional activities of the pope through which the church became more and more aware of its role as an active subject and shaper of its own history.

---

dans l'histoire de sept premiers conciles oecuméniques (Paris: Cerf, 1971); Ludwig Hertling, *Communio: Church and Papacy in Early Christianity* (Chicago: Loyola University Press, 1972).

There were several causes of this shift in paradigm. One important one was the schism between the church of the East and
the church of the West. Prior to this break, the conception of
the church that prevailed in the East was part of the universal
tradition; it was a conception marked by theological depth. For
the East, the preservation of the apostolic tradition and of the
"statutes of the fathers" remained the supreme principle. The
church was, above all else, the mystery of the body of Christ,
into which we are incorporated by baptism and the Eucharist.
The basic structure of the church remained that of a community
of local churches and, at the administrative level, the Pentarchy,
or five cooperating patriarchates, within which Rome represented
the patriarchate of the West. The Roman church and its bishop
did enjoy a special standing but not a jurisdictional precedence.
As long as the churches of the East and of the West remained
united, the East's conception of the church prevented the universal acceptance of the jurisdictional primacy claimed by the popes
as the "representatives of Peter."

The second cause of the change in paradigm was the struggle
which the popes, and especially Pope Gregory VII, were carrying
on since the beginning of the millennium for the independence of
the church and its bishops from the princes. The conflict with the
emperor and the other princes was ignited by the practice of "lay
investiture," that is, the appointment of bishops by the emperor
and the princes. The elimination of the practice was the most important goal in the Gregorian program of church reform. From
this time on, as a sign of their own "plenitude of power" over
the church, the popes had themselves crowned with the double
crown, the tiara. In this struggle of the popes for the freedom
of the church, the church became conscious of its independence
from secular rulers. The distinction was drawn between spiritual
and temporal power; this was the first step towards the modern separation of church and state. It was, above all else, this
struggle for the independence of the church that caused the popes
to insist on their universal primacy of jurisdiction. The struggle
ended only in 1122 with the Concordat of Worms, a compromise that signified a victory of the papacy. As in the eleventh

century, so also in the nineteenth, the struggle of the popes for the independence of the church was an important reason for the strengthening of the papal primacy of jurisdiction.

A further cause of the shift of paradigms in the church's self-understanding were two interconnected influences. The canonists increasingly adopted Roman law, and it was now the canonists, more than anyone else, who were deciding the definition of the church. The result was that the concept of the church became increasingly juridicized. The eucharistic ecclesiology of the church as the mystery of the body of Christ and as a *communio* receded into the background, and the discussion of the jurisdictional power of the ecclesiastical hierarchy took the limelight.

This development was reinforced by the second influence, which came from the rediscovery of Aristotle's writings on politics. These works provided a philosophy of society and a theory of law and legislative power. The body of Christ was not only a mystery of the presence of God; in this new perspective it was also a concrete social reality and, specifically, a society of human beings whose unity and independence were maintained and protected by laws. Thus the communal idea of the church's structure was replaced by a corporative conception of it. The latter developed along two lines. On the one hand, "One body — one head" led to the papal theory and to papal monarchy. On the other, "The whole body is more than each of its members" led to the conciliar theory and conciliarism.

What did this new theological paradigm of the church look like? The church as mystery of the presence of the Triune God in the body of Christ became the church that was originally established by Christ and was then entrusted to the apostles and their successors. Christ, who is priest and king, vested priests with the sacerdotal power to dispense the sacraments. To Peter and his successors he gave, in addition, the royal power of universal jurisdiction in order to lead the church. The bishops received their power of jurisdiction from the pope. This was a church of clerics and a papal monarchy.

Within this paradigm a novel conception of the papal primacy of jurisdiction developed. The development was inaugurated in

the eleventh century by Pope Gregory VII and the theologians
of the Gregorian reform. The pope who had been the shepherd
and the witness to tradition and was only secondarily to intervene to restore a violated order now became the pope who as
supreme lawgiver and judge determines and establishes the order
of the church. The central idea of Gregory VII was obedience to
God and God's order. Those who are obedient to the pope obey
God as well. This concept was the pope's decisive weapon in the
struggle for the independence of the church. Many theologians of
the Gregorian reform seemed to envisage the church as a single
diocese in which the pope appointed bishops as his representatives in ruling the separate parts. The tendency to a centralizing
conception of papal primacy was becoming clear.

Because of these developments, the opponents of Gregory VII
accused him of disregarding tradition and the inherited order of
the church, of introducing secular novelties, and of treating the
bishops as a landowner did his tenants. They were correct, for
under Gregory VII a break with the previous paradigm of church
and primacy occurred that could hardly be described as a logical
or organic development. The Gregorian reform had revolutionary
features. On the other hand, Gregory VII's views remained for
the time being a pure theory, since they could not yet be put into
practice.

The next step was taken by Pope Innocent III in the thirteenth
century. He was the first to claim to be the only "representative of
Christ" and therefore "head of the church." These two titles were
linked to the Pauline image of Christ as head of the body, which
is the church with its many members. Just as all receive from the
fullness of Christ (Jn 1:16), so all the bishops receive their power
of jurisdiction from the pope's "plenitude of power." A point
already discernible in Gregory VII now received its theological
confirmation: The pope is the source of all power of jurisdiction
in the church.

The shift from "representative of Peter" to sole "representative of Christ" was in fact a decisive step. The pope was now
no longer only the first among the successors of the apostles,
but stood over the college of bishops and the church. He rep-

resented Christ, who is placed between God and the church. Innocent's claim was given its theological basis by Bonaventure, the famous Franciscan theologian who became the most important thirteenth-century theoretician of the papal monarchy. In his view, the pope was the sole possessor of supreme and universal power of jurisdiction in the church.

Pope Innocent IV took a further step in the middle of the thirteenth century. He adopted a principle of the late Roman law, that the ruler is above the law. This step was possible because the canonists meanwhile had introduced the distinction between divine and ecclesiastical or human law. They taught that the pope is indeed subject to the divine law and cannot change the divinely appointed constitution of the church. He can, however, abrogate the human laws of the church or dispense from them, just as he can also enact new laws. Apart, therefore, from his submission to the divine law and to the divinely established constitution of the church, the pope possessed a complete freedom of action within the church. He thereby became, at least in the Roman theory, the monarch of the church.

At the end of the thirteenth century, this conception found expression in an official document, the "Profession of Faith of Michael Paleologus," which was proposed to the Byzantine emperor in 1267 by Pope Clement IV and was read out at the Second Ecumenical Council of Lyons in 1274. In this document the traditional descriptions of the primacy were supplemented by monarchical concepts:

> The Holy Roman Church possesses also the highest and full primacy and reign [*principatum*] over the universal Catholic Church, which she recognizes in truth and humility to have received with plenitude of power from the Lord himself in the person of Blessed Peter, the prince [*principe*] or head of the apostles, of whom the Roman Pontiff is the successor.... To her all the Churches are subject, their prelates give obedience and reverence to her. Her plenitude of power, moreover, is so firm that she admits the other Churches to a share in her solicitude. (ND 29)

Innocent IV thus reached the conception of a monarchical primacy of jurisdiction which the papacy and the ultramontane theologians could take up in the nineteenth century. How modern this conception was can be seen from the fact that in the sixteenth century Jean Bodin, creator of the modern theory of the state, took over the very same basic principle of Roman law that Innocent IV had adopted: The ruler is above the law (*princeps legibus solutus*). Bodin's idea of "absolute and perpetual power" is the essence of the modern concept of sovereignty and became the starting point of absolutism. As for Innocent IV the pope is bound only by divine law and the divinely established constitution of the church, so for Bodin the monarch is likewise bound only by divine and natural law and the "fundamental laws" of the state.

Until the nineteenth century Innocent IV's views met with decisive resistance in the church and were not generally accepted. The heritage of the first millennium continued to have a strong influence, and from the fourteenth century on the papacy often went through periods of weakness. In addition, the idea of an absolute monarchy was too alien to the feudal social order, with which the church was intertwined. Furthermore, from the fourteenth century on, the corporate idea of society, according to which the whole is superior to any individual, developed into a strong countercurrent even in the church.

Over and above these historical obstacles, the idea of an absolute primacy brought another problem that occupied theologians and canonists. If the pope is subject to divine law but not to the laws of the church, which he can abrogate and enact, who is responsible for seeing to it that the pope complies with divine law in the laws which he issues? The answer given by the concept of an absolute primacy is: the pope alone. The moral obligation of the church as a whole to remain faithful to binding tradition is thereby transferred to the sole conscience of the pope. This exaggeration of the idea of primacy seemed unacceptable to many since it became a source of arbitrariness and excluded every possibility of controlling or penalizing abuse. In addition, it left out of consideration the co-responsibility of the college of bishops, which had been considered part of the apostolic tradition and of the divinely ordained constitution of the church. This problem would arise for discussion during Vatican I and Vatican II.

The canonists had been discussing this problem since the eleventh century, the reason being the possibility of a heretical pope or an abusive exercise of the primacy. In view of the tension between the obligation of obedience to the divine law, on the one hand, and the authority of the pope to act in the name of the entire church, on the other, many canonists were inclined either to emphasize the limits of the papal "plenitude of power" or to link the exercise of the primacy with the obligation of consultation. The pope should seek advice from the college of cardinals or from a council. Another reason for questioning an absolute primacy was the general teaching that, especially in decrees on matters of faith, the pope possesses greater authority when he acts with a synod or council than when he acts alone. As long as people raised this question at the level of witnessing, no one thought of the pope and a council as being in competition. Only when the discussion of the question shifted to the realm of power, in the fourteenth and fifteenth centuries, did the papal power of jurisdiction and that of the council become competitors.

The Development behind the "Development" of the Primacy

This discussion among canonists shows not only the change in the church's self-understanding, within which the conception of the primacy also changed, but also the tension that arose between the paradigm of the first millennium and that of the second. The tension was between a conception of the church that understood itself exclusively as witness to a tradition which was to be preserved unchanged, and that of a church which became aware that the preservation of tradition called for action to shape this tradition.

The church had, of course, formed its own tradition from the outset, beginning with the authors of sacred scripture, then the fathers of the church, and, finally, the councils of the first millennium. The novelty was that during the second millennium the church became increasingly aware of actively shaping its tradition through decrees and laws that met the needs of the times. A sign of this growing consciousness was the distinction between divine law and ecclesiastical laws.

But if the tradition and order of the church are actively shaped by decrees and laws, the questions arise which the medieval canonists were discussing. The first question was: Who has the authority to issue decrees and enact laws: the pope alone, the pope along with the bishops, the council? The second question was that of their fidelity to the divine law or binding tradition. This now led to a new discussion on the criteria of authentic tradition and the measures by which to check and see whether these criteria were being met. During the first millennium, the age of a tradition and the consent of the witnesses were regarded as the most important criteria. During the second millennium, the authority of the possessors of jurisdiction had to be added to the list of criteria. The more the pope was understood as head of the church and as lawgiver and the more active he was in these roles, the more the question arose of his authority in decisions on matters of faith. Now we had the question of the inerrancy or infallibility of the papal magisterium. Now, too, the relationship of pope and council became a subject of contention.

Unlike the doctrine of the monarchical primacy, that of the infallibility of the papal teaching office came into existence only amid hesitation and remained disputed until Vatican I.[4] This state of affairs was not accidental, for more is at stake in defining the truth of the faith than in matters of ecclesiastical discipline and order. And then the earlier paradigm of the church as witness, as well as the consciousness of the co-responsibility of the episcopate, remained effective forces much longer in the area of the magisterium and in defining matters of faith. As a result, the question of the authority of the papal teaching office led to a much sharper confrontation between the two millen-

---

4. See Brian Tierney, *Origins of Papal Infallibility, 1150–1350* (Leiden: Brill, 1972); Ulrich Horst, *Papst-Konzil-Unfehlbarkeit: Die Ekklesiologie der Summenkommentare von Cajetan bis Billuart* (Mainz: Grünewald, 1978).

nial paradigms of the church than did the question of the papal primacy of jurisdiction. In any case, it is important to recognize that the emergence of the doctrine of papal infallibility between the twelfth and sixteenth centuries was not an accident nor was it a matter of the interests of individuals. Rather, this doctrine "developed" within the context of the development of the new paradigm of the church: The new role of the pope as monarch and lawgiver necessarily raised the question of the authoritativeness of papal teaching.

So, then, the process by which the pope was advanced to the position of monarch in the church was neither a logical nor organic development of the Petrine idea nor a consistent embodiment of the Petrine commission. This advancement was part of the growing self-consciousness of the church as being not only witness to a heritage handed down to it but also as active shaper of this inheritance or, in today's language, active subject of its own history. This was the real development which determined the so-called "development" of the Petrine office or the development behind the "development" of the papacy into a monarchical primacy. It was a one-sided development because the new self-consciousness of the church found expression only in the pope. The bishops, on the other hand, became increasingly dependent on the papal jurisdiction. Not until Vatican II would the church acknowledge that not only the pope but also the bishops and indeed every Catholic, each according to his or her vocation, is an agent in the church and plays a part in the activity of the church.[5]

This development in the church's consciousness was in turn part of the development of the individual as subject in modern Europe. The latter development began in the Middle Ages from Christian roots and led, by way of the Renaissance and humanism, to the Enlightenment, absolutism, the French Revolution, and bourgeois society.

---

5. See Hermann J. Pottmeyer, "Kontinuität und Innovation in der Ekklesiologie des II. Vatikanums," in Giuseppe Alberigo, Yves Congar, and Hermann J. Pottmeyer, eds., *Kirche im Wandel* (Düsseldorf: Patmos, 1982), 89–110.

CHAPTER THREE

The Three Traumas
of Rome on the Eve of
the First Vatican Council

The far-reaching intellectual, social, and political changes that occurred after the French Revolution had radical consequences for
the Catholic Church. The nineteenth century saw the development of modern society as we know it today. In the beginning, the
Catholic Church and the papacy were mainly a victim of the process of change. In increasing measure, however, the church took
a defensive stand against the ideas characteristic of modernity
and their consequences. The papacy placed itself in the forefront
of this fight. The First Vatican Council (1869–70) was the high
point of the struggle.

Critics have described this antimodernism as a regression to
the Middle Ages. But this is only one aspect of the reality. For
in this defensive fight against modernity the church also adopted
certain elements of modernity and thus effected a partial modern-
ization of the church itself. This observation applies especially to
the concept of the papacy. Defense against modernity by modern
means — that is the twofold nature of Vatican I.

The self-awareness of papal Rome in the nineteenth century
was shaped by three traumas. The first was ecclesial in nature;
its obsession was conciliarism, the Reformation, and Gallicanism. The second trauma was political in nature; its occasion was
the system of a state-controlled church and the French Revolution. Finally, the third trauma was intellectual and cultural; its
watchwords were rationalism, liberalism, and secularism.

The First Trauma: Conciliarism and Gallicanism

The first trauma had its origin in events of the fourteenth and fifteenth centuries, especially the Great Schism that lasted almost forty years (1378–1417). There were two, sometimes three, popes; in addition, popes and council, sometimes two councils, were in opposition. Earlier papal schisms had been overcome by "way of convention or compromise," that is, by the abdication of both popes. Since this method now failed, the only remaining solution that could save the unity of the church was the "way of a council." The Councils of Pisa (1409), Constance (1414–18), and Basel (1431–49) had finally put an end to the schism. One result of these events was the long-term weakness of the primacy.

This emergency measure in an extreme situation gave rise to a discussion on principle about the constitution of the church: Which is the court of last resort in the church? Is it the pope or a council with the pope, or is it a council, even without or against the pope if necessary? The debate led to the formation of a theory later known as conciliarism.[1] To oversimplify somewhat, there were four positions, because there were moderate and radical versions of both the papal theory and the conciliar theory. According to the *radical papal theory* the pope alone has the *plenitudo potestatis*, the "fullness of power"; all power in the church comes from the pope as the representative of Christ, so that in the case of a heretical pope or an abuse of the papacy only an intervention of God can rescue the church. The *moderate papal theory* likewise teaches the papal primacy of jurisdiction; however, it also asserts the authority of the college of bishops, which, together with the pope as its head, represents and leads the church.

The *moderate conciliar theory* is distinguished from the moderate papal theory only by the fact that in the case of the abuse

1. See Brian Tierney, *Foundations of the Conciliar Theory* (Cambridge: Cambridge University Press, 1955, 1968); Brian Tierney and Peter Linehan, eds., *Authority and Power: Studies in Medieval Law and Government* (Cambridge: Cambridge University Press, 1980); Hermann J. Sieben, *Die Konzilsidee des lateinischen Mittelalters* (Paderborn: Schöningh, 1984); Hermann J. Sieben, *Die katholische Konzilsidee von der Reformation bis zur Aufklärung* (Paderborn: Schöningh, 1988).

of office by a pope it assigns a controlling function to a council, which can expel a heretical pope from the church. The *radical conciliar theory*, or *conciliarism*, on the other hand, asserts that a council, being a unique representative of the universal church, stands in principle above the pope. Conciliarism found broad support in the Councils of Constance and Basel.[2]

Conciliar theory combines elements of the *communio* and conciliar practice of the early church with additional considerations from medieval canonical thought on the problem of a heretical pope. In the latter, a council was regarded as the most appropriate authority for determining and defining the faith of the universal church. This was supplemented by the conviction that had grown stronger since the late Middle Ages, that the needed reform of the church and the papacy was attainable only by means of a council. But it was not until the Great Schism of the fourteenth and fifteenth centuries that this theory took systematic form. The radicalization of conciliar theory in the form of conciliarism was opposed by the pope and a number of theologians.

The futile call for a council that would reform the church and the papacy, combined with conciliar theory, played an essential part in triggering the Reformation and leading to the division of the church. The papacy was neither able nor ready to give its time and attention to the important matter of necessary church reform. Only when the split had occurred did the reform Council of Trent (1545–63) take place. This council issued important reform decrees, but the debate over the constitution of the church, over the relationship between the universal church and the particular churches, and between the primacy and the episcopate remained unsettled. No consensus could be reached on these matters.[3] Thus, the elements in Rome's first trauma at the time of

2. See Antony Black, *Council and Commune: The Conciliar Movement and the Council of Basle* (Shepherdstown, W. Va.: Patmos, 1979); Klaus Schatz, *Papal Primacy from Its Origins to the Present* (Collegeville, Minn.: Liturgical Press, 1996), 100–114.

3. See Klaus Ganzer, "Gallikanische und römische Primatsauffassung im Widerstreit: Zu den ekklesiologischen Auseinandersetzungen auf dem Konzil von Trient," in *Historisches Jahrbuch* 109 (1989): 109–63.

Vatican I were the denial of the divine institution of the papal office by the reformers and conciliarism.

Although the authority of the pope grew strong once again in the post-Tridentine church, the conciliar theory, in both its moderate and its radical forms, continued to have its representatives until the early nineteenth century: in French Gallicanism and in the German imperial church episcopalism. The "Four Gallican Articles" passed by the Assembly of the French Clergy in 1682 were the Magna Carta of Gallicanism.[4] These articles played an important role in the debates at Vatican I. They declared that the pope is subordinate to a council and bound by the laws and customary rights of the universal church and the particular churches. They also declared that papal definitions of the faith are definitively irreformable only when they have received the assent of the church.

The aim in all these endeavors was to assert, against Vatican centralization, the responsibility of the college of bishops for the universal church and the authority of the individual bishops to govern their dioceses. An appeal was made to the *communio* structures of the first eight centuries of the church. The efforts were handicapped, however, by the fact that functioning collegial structures hardly existed any more. Ecumenical councils were rarely held, either because of practical difficulties or because councils were frequently in the interests neither of the papacy nor of the political powers. The episcopates in the individual countries were even more dependent politically: on the interests of princes and nobility in feudal society, and, subsequently, on the interests of the national states.

The Gallican and episcopalist efforts were thus scarcely politically innocent. When princes and governments supported the claims of the bishops against the papacy, they had an eye on their own influence in the realm of the church. Thus Gallicanism was not based solely on theological and pastoral arguments, but was often used in the service of secular power politics.

---

4. See Aimé-Georges Martimort, *Le Gallicanisme* (Paris: Presses universitaires de France, 1973).

On the other hand, neither were papal theory and Vatican centralization politically innocent. Gallicanism was, in part, a reaction to the papal claim of absolute power over the whole world, temporal as well as religious — a claim that had been given its most extreme formulation by Boniface VIII (1294–1303). The very first of the "Four Gallican Articles" rejected this claim of temporal power and insisted on the independence of the secular authority in its own sphere. Financial interests also played a role. Many of the primatial rights which the papacy claimed were linked to sizable financial demands. Finally, the papacy and the princes were at odds over the right to appoint bishops, because this was a matter of great political importance.

By now it is clear how much questions of the church's constitution were connected with political situations and interests. This is not surprising in a society in which the Christian religion and the entire social and political life were so interrelated, and in which the influence of the church was felt everywhere; a more exact distinction between secular and spiritual authority was still far from being worked out. But there was more involved than simply the immediate influence of secular politics. The debates on the constitution of the church also reflected long-term social and political developments. The influence of secular models of social and political order could be seen in concepts within the church's constitution. There were clear parallels in this area.

First, then, was the parallel with feudal society during the high Middles Ages. The feudal social order in Europe saw a plurality of rulers. Although these were arranged in a hierarchical order, even subordinate rulers had a certain independence. There was a similar ecclesiastical order that included both the hierarchical supremacy of the pope and the independent responsibility of bishops for their dioceses.[5]

Beginning in the fourteenth century, the corporate model of society developed alongside the feudal model. According to this new model, which appeared most clearly in the cities, universi-

---

5. See Kenneth Pennington, *Pope and Bishops: The Papal Monarchy in the Twelfth and Thirteenth Centuries* (Philadelphia: University of Pennsylvania Press, 1984).

ties, and mendicant orders, the *universitas,* or entire corporation, held supreme authority, exercised by an elected body. The elected leader, or *rector,* was superior to individuals but not to the *universitas;* rather, he was the latter's representative. At the level of the state this model took form in the parliaments, in which the king collaborated with the three estates — the clergy, the nobility, and the peasants and burghers — in passing laws and financing the state. In the realm of the church the corporate model was reflected in conciliarism. According to the latter, the pope was superior to all the members of the church, but not to the church in its entirety, which was represented by a council. Laws or definitions of faith issued by the pope became valid only when received by the entire church. This was the model to which the "Four Gallican Articles" were adapted.

The Second Trauma: The System of a State-Controlled Church

The second trauma for the nineteenth-century papacy was what became known as the system of state control of the church. This led to the extensive dependence of the bishops on monarchs and on the state bureaucracy.

There were three main causes of the rise of this system beginning in the fourteenth century: the weakness of the papacy as a result of the Great Schism; the rise of the French king and other monarchs to the position of absolute rulers; and, finally, the confessional civil wars of the sixteenth and seventeenth centuries.

After the Great Schism, many princes began to exercise oversight and control of the church in their territory. In France the "Four Gallican Articles" became the law of the state. The French model of a state-controlled church then became a model for the whole of Europe. It was here that the alliance of "Throne and Altar" was forged, in which the church profited from the protection of the king and the king made use of the church for his own purposes. Later on, this alliance brought upon the church the reproach, from revolutionary and liberal forces, of being inseparably tied to a political order on its way out. The papacy had never accepted the limits set to its primacy by the system of a state-controlled church, but for the time being it was unable to assert its claims.

The state-controlled church system was strengthened by the rise of absolutist monarchies, for which France again provided the model. This development was promoted in turn by the confessional civil wars. Since the nation was confessionally divided, the king became the only power that could establish peace and order. The mark of an absolutist monarchy was that the monarch alone possessed supreme ruling authority and was not dependent in its exercise on the cooperation and agreement of the estates and their representatives. The absolutist monarch was above the laws passed by legislatures and could even break them. He was, however, morally bound by the divine and natural law and what were historically the "basic laws" of the monarchy; it was this that distinguished an absolutist monarchy from despotism and totalitarianism. The absolutist monarchies that existed in individual European countries until the middle of the nineteenth century kept the church in their countries dependent on the state.

The defenders of the papal theory took the model of the absolute monarch and applied it to the primacy of the pope to express his supreme authority. The concept of *sovereignty*, which the theoreticians of absolutist monarchy had been developing since the sixteenth century into a central concept in the modern theory of the state, was a concept that played an important part in the application of the model of the absolute monarch to papal primacy.[6]

Since that time, sovereignty has been understood as the supreme, absolute, indivisible power of the state to rule and issue decrees without dependence on any other consent or confirmation. In an absolutist monarchy sovereignty resides in the monarch; later on, in the democracies, it will reside in the people. *External* sovereignty means independence from other

---

6. See Hermann J. Pottmeyer, *Unfehlbarkeit und Souveränität: Die päpstliche Unfehlbarkeit im System der ultramontanen Ekklesiologie des 19. Jahrhunderts* (Mainz: Grünewald, 1975), 346–409.

states; *internal* sovereignty means the independence of the supreme authority from any other power within the state.

In the nineteenth century the concept of sovereignty was increasingly applied to the primacy of the pope. The basis of this application was a concept in Roman law: *plenitudo potestatis* or "the fullness of power." The popes had already been taking advantage of this concept for a long time, and the first absolute monarchs also appealed to it. It was from this concept that many theoreticians of the papacy derived the doctrine that all authority in the church, even that of the bishops, has its source in the papal primacy. This corresponded exactly to the modern concept of sovereignty, which acknowledges no plurality of powers.

The concept of sovereignty had a twofold advantage for the primacy. Appealing to his external sovereignty, the pope could claim his independence of princes and states; by reason of his internal sovereignty he could claim a position of absolute independence in relation to councils and bishops within the church. This concept was thus a suitable means of rejecting, on the one hand, conciliarism and Gallicanism, and, on the other, state control of the church and other limitations on the primacy by the states.

The success of this concept can be seen in the fact that the pope was more and more named as "Sovereign Pontiff." There was also a famous incident during Vatican I, when Pius IX in the course of a lively discussion said: "La tradizione sono io!" ("I am tradition!") or, according to another source, "La Chiesa sono io!" ("I am the church!"). This paralleled the remark of the French king Louis XIV, who was the prototype of an absolute monarch: "L'État c'est moi!" ("I am the state!").[7]

Thus it was the struggle for the freedom of the church that seemed to demand an absolute primacy and a centralized government of the church. Conciliar theory and Gallicanism seemed to be necessarily disavowed as being the gateway to the system of state control of the church. In any case, this last was the view of a movement that increasingly gained adherents and

---

7. See Klaus Schatz, *Vaticanum I* (Paderborn: Schöningh, 1994), 3:312–22.

influence in the nineteenth century: *ultramontanism*. This movement was called "ultramontane," because it looked entirely to
Rome, i.e., beyond the Alps from the viewpoint of France and
Germany, and encouraged strengthening papal primacy. The concern of the ultramontane movement and its triumphal march are
easily explained.[8]

The French Revolution of 1789 had destroyed the existing social and political order in France. The ecclesiastical order was
likewise radically affected. Napoleon drew almost the whole of
Europe into this process of change. Through the "Civil Constitution" of 1790 the Parisian National Assembly, acting in the name
of the sovereignty of the people, made the French church radically subordinate to the state. In 1799 Pius VI died in prison,
having been dragged off to France in humiliating fashion and
to the horror of Catholics. In 1801, his successor, Pius VII, was
able to conclude a concordat with Napoleon that was to restore
the ecclesiastical order in France. In 1802, however, Napoleon
unilaterally added the "Organic Articles" to the concordat, thus
making the four Gallican Articles once again official teaching in
France and renewing state control of the church. The restored
monarchy in France held to this arrangement even after the fall
of Napoleon.

After 1803, many European states likewise introduced a state-
church system in which the church was subordinated to the state
bureaucracy. After persistent negotiations the papacy did succeed
in ensuring certain rights for Catholics by means of concordats
with the various governments. Nonetheless, a state-controlled
church system remained in place in many European states until
the end of the nineteenth century and, in some places, even into
the twentieth.

In light of all this, the rise of the ultramontane movement in
the nineteenth century was not surprising. Initially, it did not
come from either the episcopate or the papacy. In 1856, Alexis
de Tocqueville observed: "It was a matter more of the pope be-

---

8. See E. E. Y. Hales, *Revolution and Papacy* (New York: Doubleday, 1960);
G. McCool, *Catholic Theology in the Nineteenth Century* (New York: Seabury,
1977).

ing compelled by the faithful to become absolute master of the church than of the faithful being compelled by him to become his subordinates. Rome's attitude was an effect rather than a cause."[9] It was young priests and laypersons who placed themselves at the head of the movement, fought for the independence of the church, and called for the external and internal sovereignty of the pope. For an ever-growing number of the faithful the pope was the sole guarantor of ecclesiastical independence. Social upheavals caused them to see the pope as the protector and renewer of the ecclesiastical and social orders. An emotional devotion to the pope, such as had never existed before, was the reaction to the profound humiliation of the papacy by Napoleon and to the attitude of hostility to pope and church on the part of many governments and of liberalism. With the accession of Gregory XIV as pope in 1831, the papacy placed itself at the head of the ultramontane movement.[10]

The Third Trauma: Rationalism and Liberalism

The third trauma that influenced the thought and action of the papacy in the nineteenth century was the loss of authority which the faith and the church suffered since the Enlightenment. Christianity, theology, and the papacy had, as late as the early modern age, shown themselves open to the sciences and the humanities and capable of assimilating them. Now the development of the sciences and the humanities was so great an intellectual challenge to the traditional understanding of the faith that it led to conflict.

The cause was not simply specific items of knowledge in the natural sciences and history that questioned the authority of the Bible and its interpretation by the church. A new self-understanding of human beings also developed along with the sciences. People claimed autonomy, and this for the activity both of their reason and of their freedom, understood as the power of

---

9. In Emile Ollivier, *L'église et l'état au Concile du Vatican* (Paris, 1879), 314.

10. See J. Derek Holmes, *The Triumph of the Holy See* (Shepherdstown, W. Va.: Patmos, 1978).

self-determination. People also subjected all the previously prevailing traditions and authorities to their criticism. The church's
response of rejection strengthened the representatives of progress
in their conviction that progress would win out only if it opposed the church and, ultimately, religion. To the extent that
progressives saw religion as their most important enemy, faith in
progress through science and revolution often developed into an
anti-Christian religion. The growing claim of modern human beings to shape the world and take control of their personal destiny
had its roots originally in the Jewish-Christian tradition. Now,
ironically, it became increasingly difficult for the church to accept
these claims.

We are well informed about how the papacy, and many
bishops and theologians as well, viewed this development. The
encyclicals of Popes Gregory XVI and Pius IX and the records
and documents of Vatican I clearly testify to their views.[11] As
they saw it, the common characteristic of all modern errors was
rationalism, the cult of autonomous reason, which claimed primacy and rejected every other authority, even that of God and
the church. Rationalism led of necessity to the denial of God's
existence, or atheism. Closely connected to rationalism was naturalism, the cult of a pure this-worldliness, which replaced faith
in God with faith in scientific and social progress. Naturalism
and empiricism were followed by materialism, which denied the
spiritual nature of the human person. In fact, it even called into
question reason itself and its fundamental truths. The consequences were relativism and indifferentism. Fundamental in all
these evils was the Reformation, because it had substituted the
private judgment of the individual for the authority of the church.
It was there that the modern claim to the autonomy of human
beings and their reason and freedom had its origin. Liberalism,
which spread this claim in the intellectual and political spheres,
was, as the popes saw it, nothing but a rejection of the authority
of God and the church.

---

11. See Hermann J. Pottmeyer, *Der Glaube vor dem Anspruch der Wissenschaft*
(Freiburg: Herder, 1968), 17–45; Klaus Schatz, *Vaticanum I* (Paderborn: Schöningh, 1993), 2:81–94.

Gregory XVI and Pius IX carried on an increasingly energetic struggle against all these errors. All the efforts of Catholic theologians and philosophers to enter into a dialogue with the modern world likewise fell victim to that sweeping judgment. And Catholics who, in the interests of the freedom of the church, tried to reconcile the church with the freedom movements of the age and with their justifiable concerns suffered the same fate. All such attempts were bound to fail because Rome staked everything on a single cause: the restoration of the principle of authority within church and society.

In this traumatized perspective, priority was given to the strengthening of the primacy and authority of the pope.[12] The fact that the popes, beginning with Gregory XVI, took over the leadership of the ultramontane movement was connected not only with the struggle against the state-controlled church system but even more with the struggle against modern "errors." The popes understood themselves and their teaching authority to be the most important bulwark against the penetration of modern thought into the church. The most drastic expression of this self-understanding was the "Syllabus" of 1864, the list of modern errors which Pius IX published two days after the announcement of Vatican Council I. In the papacy's intention, this council was to make the "Syllabus" its own and turn it into dogma, along with the infallibility of the papal magisterium.

The Papacy between Rejection of Modernity and Modernization

The European events and developments which I have outlined above explain the climate at the time of Vatican I and the driving forces behind it. Because many Catholics and the papacy itself felt these political and scientific developments to be threatening

---

12. See Maurice Nédoncelle, Roger Aubert, and Yves Congar, eds., *L'ec-clésiologie au XIXe siècle* (Paris: Cerf, 1960); Yves Congar, "The Historical Development of Authority in the Church," in John M. Todd, ed., *Problems of Authority* (Baltimore: Helicon, 1962), 119–56.

and even traumatic, the council was put on the defensive. The principle of authority should become, as the pope and the majority of the council fathers saw it, the church's most important bastion against the modern world. The authority of the pope had to be strengthened in order to restore it. It is important to understand that in the eyes of many the threat to Christianity and the church had taken on almost apocalyptic dimensions. In view of this threat it was thought that rescue could come only from the pope and a centralized exercise of his primacy.

Whether or not, as we look back from our present vantage point, we share the estimate made of the situation at the time, it does in any case explain the fact that the primacy and authority of the pope were formulated by Vatican I in a consciously one-sided way. This deliberate one-sidedness — which, however, was not intended to change anything in the original constitution of the church as sanctified by tradition — is an important point for the interpretation and assessment of Vatican I.

Another important point is the fact that due to the one-sided emphasis on papal primacy since Gregory XVI, the Petrine office took on a new form. The theory of an absolute papal monarchy had already been drafted back in the thirteenth and fourteenth centuries, but in the context of a Catholic society that was, at that time, feudal in its structure. This conception of the papacy was able to reappear only in the late nineteenth century, after the French Revolution and Napoleon had gotten rid of the feudal structures that had supported the claim of the episcopate to its own rights. In addition, it was now possible to take the absolutist monarchies as a model and to formulate papal power as sovereignty. The context in which this was done, however, was no longer a society that was coextensive with the Catholic Church, but the world of developing national states which no longer acknowledged the higher authority of the pope. The distinction between church and state had now become clearer, and even the papacy insisted on it in its struggle against the state-dominated church system. The primacy of the pope now existed only within the Catholic Church, but there it was absolute.

Until Vatican I, however, an important element had been lacking in the sovereignty of the pope. As a primacy of jurisdiction it extended to the realm of ecclesiastical discipline. But until the council there was disagreement over whether the pope could also act as a sovereign in the area of doctrine. For it was the general conviction of tradition and church law that in matters of faith a council was more than the pope alone, and that an individual pope could become a heretic and, in this case, be condemned and deposed by a council or otherwise. The infallibility of the church in faith and doctrine was tied to the consensus of the entire church, which a council represented. Since that tradition was now seen as a limitation on the absolute sovereignty of the pope, the definition of papal infallibility became an important element in the program of the ultramontane movement.[13] Conflict arose on this point at Vatican I.

When seen in a sociological perspective, the events[1] outlined above were part of the process of development of modern society. Sociologists speak of a "churchification" of Christianity that began in the nineteenth century and reached its culmination in the twentieth.[14] The church in Europe could no longer rely on emperor and kings as "defenders of the faith" or count on feudal structures to safeguard its independence. Rather it had to rely on its own structures if it were to be present in society without becoming dependent on the state. Elements in this modernizing remodelling of the church included the organizing of the laity in Catholic societies and associations, the building of systems of Catholic schools and hospitals, and, of course, the centralization of the government of the church in the hands of the "Sovereign Pontiff." The development of papal primacy on the model of the absolute monarch is in fact nothing less than a modernizing of the papacy to the level of the early modern age, just as feudalism had been superseded by absolutism. With the end of the papal states immediately after Vatican I, the papacy, too, lost its feudal basis. But it no longer needed this, since in the meantime the

---

13. See Richard F. Costigan, *Rohrbacher and the Ecclesiology of Ultramontanism* (Rome: Gregoriana, 1980).

14. See Franz-Xaver Kaufmann, *Kirche begreifen* (Freiburg: Herder, 1979), 100–110.

council had turned papal primacy into a dogma and had thereby ensured its practical acceptance within the Catholic Church.

The further development of political forms in Europe has had no effect on the form of the papacy. It has adhered to the early modern model of the absolute monarch. In the majority of European states, however, the course of the nineteenth century saw the development of the constitutional monarchy, which combines prerevolutionary forms of participation with liberal ideas. However, all the proposals of reform theologians to return to forms of participation characteristic of the early church and the Middle Ages have foundered on the threefold trauma of Rome.

CHAPTER FOUR

Vatican I and Papal Primacy of Jurisdiction

Primacy as Sovereignty

A book that appeared in 1799 can help us grasp the concept of jurisdictional primacy that arose in the nineteenth century, as well as the novel character of this concept. Although the book appeared during a period when the papacy was deeply humiliated, it bore the title of *The Triumph of the Holy See and the Church over the Attacks of Innovators, Who Are Rejected and Fought with Their Own Weapons.* The author was a Camaldolese monk, Mauro Cappellari (1765–1846).[1] His book was a response to a work that had appeared in 1784: *The Authentic Idea of the Holy See,* by Pietro Tamburini, who associated conciliarist and Gallican concepts with the idea of popular sovereignty and democracy. Cappellari's book was to mark a new epoch, because in 1831 its author became Pope Gregory XVI, and he began to put into practice his own conception of primacy.

The first novelty of Cappellari's book was its reasoning. In order to substantiate their position, whether Gallican or ultramontane, theologians had previously appealed to the testimonies of tradition. Cappellari declared that it was not necessary to get involved in the confusion of antiquity and go back to the time of the apostles. Christ, he said, had given the church a form of

---

1. Mauro Cappellari, *Il trionfo della Santa Sede e della Chiesa contro gli assalti de' novatori respinti e combattuti colle stesse loro armi* (Rome, 1799); see Ulrich Horst, *Unfehlbarkeit und Geschichte: Studien zur Unfehlbarkeitsdiskussion von Melchior Cano bis zum 1. Vatikanischen Konzil* (Mainz: Grünewald, 1982), 78–120.

government that had remained unchanged in its external form
down to the present time. It was therefore possible to determine
from the present form of government what its permanently valid
form is.

This was a revolutionary step, and one that took the paradigm
followed in the first millennium and turned it on its head. While
the first millennium preserved the ancient tradition unchanged
by adapting itself to the testimonies of this tradition, Cappellari
simply took the immutability of the tradition for granted and declared the study of the testimonies to it to be unnecessary. He
interpreted the tradition exclusively in the light of the present:
What is today has always been.

Cappellari's intention in arguing thus was to put an end to the
discussion of how to test and make certain the legitimacy of measures taken by the papacy. His only interest was in securing the
sovereignty of papal activity. He thus carried to an extreme the
paradigm that dominated in the second millennium (the church as
active subject and shaper of its own history) and annulled the first
millennium's justified concern to respect the authority of tradition. The only thing important and decisive now was the present
and its requirements.

Novel, too, was the explicit assertion of the analogy between
church and state. Cappellari criticizes the claim that the authority of the church is effective only due to the force of conviction
and because it completely lacks the spirit of domination. On the
contrary, he says, the right of legitimate domination, which is not
to be confused with despotism, is appropriate for the church, no
less than for the state. He argued that those who deny the church
this right foster a spiritualization of the church and leave it open
to encroachments by civil authority. Here we can see at work the
trauma inflicted by a system in which the state dominated the
church.

The analogy with the modern state made it possible for Cappellari to adopt the concept of sovereignty. God, being himself the
"sovereign ruler" of the church, has given to the church, in the
person of the pope, a sovereign government. The pope's sovereign
plenitude of power includes legislative, judicial, and executive au-

thority and can demand unqualified obedience. The "Sovereign Pontiff" is independent both abroad and domestically. Cappellari thus explicitly described papal primacy of jurisdiction in terms of the modern concept of sovereignty; he also demanded recognition of papal infallibility as a necessary condition of his sovereignty.

According to Cappellari, if people understood primacy to mean sovereignty, all the disagreements between Gallicans and ultramontanists would be settled. It now appeared superfluous to discuss whether the consent of the church, the advice of the cardinals, or the cooperation of the episcopal college must play a part in papal decisions. Furthermore, such discussions would only confuse the faithful. Guidance by a simple and clear authority was needed to ensure steadfastness in the faith, and only the voice of Peter could supply this guidance. This reasoning is reminiscent of the arguments of the theoreticians of the authoritarian state. Once Gregory XVI took office, this book was published widely in the most important languages.

In fact, the conception of papal primacy as sovereignty became one of the central ideas of the ultramontanist movement. Among the leading thinkers of this movement were Joseph de Maistre (1753–1821) and Félicité Lamennais (1782–1854). De Maistre was a legal scholar and the ideologue behind the restoration of the French monarchy after the fall of Napoleon. His aim was to establish the divine right of kings and restore the unity of throne and altar. Because God is a sovereign ruler, he argued, so too must every monarch be a sovereign ruler. God's sovereignty on earth is represented first of all by the Sovereign Pontiff. De Maistre's book *Du Pape* (The pope) appeared in 1819; in it (whether with a knowledge of Cappellari's work or independent of it), he developed his theory of papal sovereignty.[2]

> Christianity rests entirely on the pope, so that the principles of
> the political and social order...may be derived from the following
> chain of reasoning: there can be no public morality and no national
> character without religion, no European religion without Christian-

---

2. Joseph de Maistre, *Du Pape* (Lyon, 1819; Geneva, 1966).

ity, no Christianity without Catholicism, no Catholicism without the
pope, no pope without sovereignty that belongs to him.[3]

De Maistre's book became very influential. The most important thing about it was that he defined papal primacy as absolute
and infallible sovereignty. Charles de Montalembert wrote in
1852: "The ideas expressed by the great Count de Maistre in
his book on the pope became self-evident to all Catholic young
people."[4]

Lamennais was a representative of the younger generation and
one who exerted no little influence. Unlike de Maistre, his sole
concern was the freedom of the church, but, like de Maistre,
he defined papal primacy as sovereignty that included the infallibility of the pope. In Lamennais's view, this sovereignty was the
basis of the independence of the church from the state. The more
Gregory XVI and Pius IX turned in a restorational and antiliberal
direction, the more Lamennais became an opponent of the papacy, for he saw, correctly, that in the long run the freedom of the
church could be secured only within a society based on freedom.[5]

Although de Maistre and Lamennais were pursuing primarily
political goals, they prepared the way for Cappellari's theological ideas to become increasingly influential after 1831. These
ideas, however, represented nothing less than a break with previous tradition and the previous conception of primacy and with
the traditional communal order of the church. Cappellari did
not indeed deny that the episcopal college, along with the pope,
has universal jurisdictional authority and responsibility. But the
"use" of this universal jurisdictional authority by the episcopal
college is dependent, according to Cappellari, entirely on the initiative and permission of the pope, to whom all owe absolute
obedience. He thereby stripped collegial jurisdictional authority
of its legal effectiveness, in favor of a papal monopoly based upon
sovereign jurisdiction. True enough, even Cappellari rejected any

---

3. Joseph de Maistre, Letter to the Count of Blacas, in *Correspondance IV*
(Lyon, 1821), 428.

4. In Emile Ollivier, *L'église et l'état au Concile du Vatican* (Paris, 1879), 315.

5. See B. Reardon, *Liberalism and Tradition: Aspects of Catholic Thought in
Nineteenth Century France* (Cambridge: Cambridge University Press, 1975).

papal despotism, since the pope is bound by divine law. However, the bishops would have no way of resisting a despotic or heretical pope except by rebelling or by praying for a divine intervention since he provided no institutional way in which the bishops could regularly exercise their universal responsibility except with the permission of the pope. Cappellari's position went a step beyond that of the thirteenth century because it claimed the pope's infallibility was an element in his sovereignty.

The break with the inherited tradition and order of the church consisted, then, in the fact that Cappellari excluded the responsibility of the episcopate for the universal church, not indeed in theory, but in practice. The break was a deliberate one for, in his argument, he declared any consideration of the testimonies of tradition to be completely irrelevant. On the eve of Vatican I the conception of papal primacy as indivisible sovereignty was regarded by many as traditional teaching, whereas it was a very new idea.

This undifferentiated and authoritarian conception of the primacy did not meet with universal acceptance in the nineteenth century, however. Even within the ultramontane movement, voices were raised expressing reservations or criticisms. Among these critics were many bishops whose understanding of their office was rooted in tradition and who did not regard themselves as functionaries of the pope. Then there were the voices of many theologians who took a more nuanced position on the relationship between primacy, the episcopate, and the church. In addition, there were Catholic leaders who, whether moderately ultramontane or moderately liberal, spoke up for a reconciliation between the church and the modern world and who, therefore, were critical of authoritarian papal rule or simply rejected it. Finally, we may not overlook the fact that many Catholics had a great veneration for, and attachment to, the pope, because it was to the pope that they looked for a strengthening of the church and the defense of their own rights against the bureaucracy of the state. Certainly, they did not want an authoritarian church.

One thing became clear in all the discussions among bishops and theologians that became increasingly tense on the eve of Vat-

ican I: Those who spoke in favor of a balance between primacy
and the episcopate were confronted with the ultramontane objection that they were seeking to divide the indivisible sovereignty
of the pope. The defenders of papal sovereignty rejected (as a
dividing-up of papal sovereignty) any obligation on the part of
the pope to consult or any right of the episcopate to share in
the work. This was true even though defenders of papal sovereignty could not deny that the episcopate possesses, together with
the pope, a responsibility for, and jurisdiction over, the universal
church. Thus the understanding of primacy of jurisdiction as a
form of sovereignty proved to be the real obstacle to agreement
among the partners in the discussion. The same was to become
clear in the debates at the council.

Both sides were unaware of the fact that those who appealed
to the tradition in behalf of greater episcopal collaboration with
the pope were implicitly appealing to the paradigm of the first
millennium, that is, to the church as a community of witnesses.
The defenders of absolute sovereignty, however, were arguing
one-sidedly within the context of the paradigm of the second
millennium.

The Proposal of a "Complex Sovereignty"

The most interesting position taken in preconciliar discussion
was that of one of the most outstanding French theologians of
the nineteenth century, namely, Bishop Henri Maret, dean of
the theological faculty of the Sorbonne.[6] His book, *Du concile
général et de la paix religieuse* (General council and religious
peace) appeared in 1869, three months before the council, and set
off a vehement discussion. The book was a penetrating critique of
de Maistre and his conception of primacy as absolute monarchy.
In contrast to de Maistre, Maret wanted a reconciliation of the
church with the modern world.

---

6. See Klaus Schatz, "Eine 'gallikanische' Interpretation des Unfehlbarkeits-
dogmas: Die Rezeption des 1. Vatikanums durch Bischof Maret," *Theologie und
Philosophie* 59 (1984): 499–534.

First, Maret's critique of de Maistre. Maret criticized the "absolutist school" because, he said, it granted the pope pure and simple, indivisible, absolute, and unlimited sovereignty. According to de Maistre, the church is a monarchy "pure and simple," because there is nothing in the church in addition to, and above, the pope. It is an "indivisible" monarchy because de Maistre excludes any participation whatever in the government of the universal church. It is an "absolute" monarchy because the pope alone makes laws and demands absolute obedience to his laws. Finally, it is an "unlimited" monarchy because, according to de Maistre, the pope is answerable only to God.[7]

The heart of the absolutist idea, according to Maret, was that it made the pope the sole source of episcopal jurisdiction. Since the pope is above all ecclesiastical laws and need consult only his own conscience, the way is opened to arbitrariness. The only thing the pope cannot decree is the abolition of the episcopate, but in any case he becomes the absolute master of episcopal jurisdiction.[8] In this description Maret reported very accurately the idea of absolute sovereignty as found in de Maistre.

In order to refute de Maistre's conception of the primacy, Maret investigated the history and structure of the councils, for it is in them that the divinely given constitution of the church is most clearly seen. Just as Peter and the other apostles formed a "collective unit,"[9] so the pope and the bishops do at a council. Sovereignty belongs, therefore, Maret argued, neither to the pope alone nor to the episcopate alone.[10] At a council pope and bishops reach a joint decision after joint consultation; the same pattern should be followed outside councils in the making of laws for the entire church. In support of this view, Maret developed the concept of a "composite sovereignty" or "complex sovereignty."[11] The pope possesses primacy of jurisdiction only as head of the college of bishops. It depends on him alone "how"

---

7. Henri Maret, *Du concile général et de la paix religieuse* (Paris, 1869), 1:130.
8. Ibid., 2:10.
9. Ibid., 1:137.
10. Ibid., 1:341.
11. Ibid., 1:335.

he discerns the consent of the bishops. But the legislative sovereignty is shared by the pope with the bishops.[12] Maret thus made
a distinction between primacy of jurisdiction and the concept of
sovereignty.

Maret found the idea of "complex sovereignty" given concrete
form in the conciliar practice of the church. He saw correctly
that joint witness was the basis of councils as an institution.[13]
The popes were, in fact, obliged to accept the joint witness of
the churches and their bishops testifying to the binding tradition. However, in councils the bishops were not only witnesses
but judges who made decisions binding on the entire church; this
way of acting could be extended, in Maret's view, to the making
of laws even outside the councils.

Maret realized, quite correctly, that the definition of jurisdictional primacy as absolute sovereignty of the pope threatened to
change the original constitution of the church. True enough, this
conception of the primacy did not amount to a theological denial of the divine right of the episcopate, but it did deprive the
co-responsibility of the bishops for the entire church of any legal
effectiveness. Maret also realized that collegial co-responsibility
of the bishops in the postfeudal church could find effective expression only if the bishops shared in the making of laws for the
universal church. Finally, he recognized that the right to make
laws was an essential element in the concept of sovereignty. For
this reason, he extended the concept of sovereignty to the entire
college of bishops, together with the pope as its head.

Maret intended by his proposal to do justice to the original constitution and practice of the church. His proposal also
gave expression to his other concern, namely, to reconcile the
church with the modern world. In Maret's time, modern developments in traditional constitutions advanced society beyond
absolute monarchy to constitutional monarchy. Included in the
idea of constitutional monarchy was the sharing of sovereignty
and the effective check by parliament on the power of the execu-

---

12. Ibid., 1:341.
13. Ibid., 2:416f.

tive. In Maret's view, papal despotism, which even his opponents rejected, could not be avoided unless laws binding the entire church became operative only after joint consultation and with the prior, or subsequent, agreement of the bishops. Maret's intention was that by sharing fully in the government of the church the bishops should be an effective check on the exercise of papal primacy of jurisdiction. The sharing of the episcopate in making laws and in an effective check on power were, according to Maret, elements in the constitution of the church that corresponded to constitutional developments of participation in the secular sphere.

Maret's proposal ran into sharp criticism from the ultramontanists. Their primary concern was that the pope should be independent and free to act, so as to make his authority more effective. This is why they defined primacy of jurisdiction as absolute sovereignty of the pope. They were, therefore, forced to reject any sharing of this sovereignty. They criticized Maret for making the exercise of jurisdictional primacy dependent on the consent of the bishops. In their view, the pope would become a mere agent for carrying out majority decisions of the episcopate, and the bishops would become co-sharers in the primacy of jurisdiction.

This criticism was justified, for, in fact, Maret's proposal amounted to making the exercise of jurisdictional primacy dependent unilaterally on the consent of the bishops. Traditional doctrine said that supreme governmental authority in the church is exercised both by the pope and by the college of bishops together with the pope. This governmental structure means that both agents, or both ways, of exercising supreme authority are indeed related each to the other, but are not dependent one on the other. How this unique governmental structure functions was a question that the Council of Trent had been unable to resolve in the past, and it would again occupy the Second Vatican Council. Maret's proposal to conceive of this unique governmental structure as a "complex sovereignty" was doubtless a suggestion worth discussing, but inasmuch as it meant sharing of sovereignty, it did not do justice to the special position of the pope.

Conversely, the ultramontane position, which assigned the pope an absolute sovereignty, did not do justice to the important role of the college of bishops.

In any case, Maret raised some interesting questions that pointed towards the future. Maret's critics were wrong in describing his views as Gallican. For Gallicanism, at least in its original form, was a mix of elements from the early church and feudalism. In fact, Maret's proposal was connected with an entirely new and modern question. This fact emerges only when we recall the difference between the paradigms of the first and second millennia. In his proposal Maret appealed to the conciliar practice of the first millennium, which aimed at jointly testifying to the ancient tradition and strengthening its binding character. The order and the laws of the church formed part of this tradition. Pope and bishops subordinated themselves to ancient tradition and to the ancient order in the church.

In the second millennium, on the other hand, the focus increasingly came to be placed on regulating the life of the church by means of new laws. And it was the pope who increasingly understood himself to be the sole lawgiver of the church. Maret now asked the right question: whether legislating for the universal church is not a task of the college of bishops together with the pope rather than of the pope alone. This question had not arisen as long as the popes intervened in the life of the church in only a secondary way, that is, in order to safeguard or restore the ancient order, and as long as they reserved only certain privileges to themselves. However, when the popes increasingly regulated the life of the church by means of universally binding laws, their activity increasingly impacted on the inherent rights of the bishops in their dioceses, as well as on the general well-being and life of the entire church. Nor was this activity any longer concerned simply with preserving the ancient order; instead, new laws were being issued. Was it therefore not appropriate for the bishops to share, in some way, in the making of these laws?

In asking this question Maret was far ahead of his time. The concern he voiced played little part in the discussions of Vatican I, but it did in the debates of Vatican II. Maret was thus asking a new question, one that was typical of the paradigm of the church in the second millennium. If the pope was increasingly establishing himself as the active subject in the shaping of the church's life, what about the bishops and their role as responsible agents in the church?

Bishop Maret's position, insofar as it suggested a sharing of sovereignty or of the papal primacy of jurisdiction, was condemned by Vatican I when it stated: "If anyone says that he [the Roman Pontiff] has only a more important part and not the complete fullness of his supreme power...*anathema sit*" (ND 830).

The Conciliar Debate

Anyone familiar with the prehistory of Vatican I could legitimately expect the council to define the primacy of jurisdiction as an absolute, monarchical sovereignty of the pope. This was also the expectation of the representatives of an extreme ultramontanism and of Pius IX himself. But anyone reading the definitive conciliar text makes a surprising discovery: One finds that this expectation is not borne out. The text of the council is undoubtedly marked by the atmosphere of its time, but it does *not* define the primacy of jurisdiction as an absolute, monarchical sovereignty as understood by Cappellari and de Maistre.[14]

This realization is very important for the interpretation of the definition issued by Vatican I. People are often satisfied to cite only the text of the definition. The only thing that can be seen then is the one-sided emphasis on the papal primacy of jurisdiction. But if we look at the definition against the background of the original, extreme ultramontanist proposal, we are struck by its relative moderation. The maximalist interpretation of Vatican I, indeed, gives a one-sidedly ultramontanist explanation of the definition of primacy of jurisdiction. One ploy used by

14. See Patrick Granfield, *The Limits of the Papacy: Authority and Autonomy in the Church* (New York: Crossroad, 1987); James Hennesey, *The First Council of the Vatican: The American Experience* (New York: Herder and Herder, 1963).

maximizing interpreters consisted in treating whatever was not expressly stated in the definition as nonexistent. But the Vatican I council fathers saw the relationship between pope and bishops as more nuanced. In order to be clear on this, we must study the discussions that took place at Vatican I.

It is not possible here to review in detail the genesis of the text and the discussion of it at the First Vatican Council. But some observations must be made that are important for its interpretation.

In the preparatory dogmatic commission that had to compose the draft of a text on the church, the ultramontanist idea of an absolute papal monarchy clearly prevailed.[15] The pope was described as monarch of the church, the bishops as princes subordinate to him.[16] Above all, there was an emphasis on the "absolute independence" of papal primacy, which in its exercise has no limits except those set by divine and natural law and by the welfare of the church.[17] All the same, one of the consultors remarked that it would be prudent not to lay such stress on the freedom and independence of papal authority as to make it seem despotic.[18] At this point, too, there were repeated objections to describing papal authority as "ordinary and immediate," because this expression gave the impression that the jurisdiction of the bishops in their dioceses was being swallowed up by the authority of the pope.[19] Thus there was a determination, from the outset, not to deny or weaken the authority proper to the bishops.

In January 1870, the draft text of the preparatory commission was given to the council fathers for their written comments.[20] There was general agreement with the statement that the pope possesses full and supreme jurisdictional authority over the en-

---

15. See Gustave Thils, *La primauté pontificale: La doctrine de Vatican I, les voies d'une revision* (Gembloux: Duculot, 1972), 18–43; Klaus Schatz, *Vaticanum I* (Paderborn: Schöningh, 1992), 1:149–55.

16. See Thils, *La primauté* 46, n. 3.

17. Ibid., 45, 54.

18. M 49, 667A.

19. M 49, 574 BC, 708 C.

20. M 51, 929 B–972 D.

tire church. At the same time, many of the council fathers were critical of the fact that the bishops and their rights were passed over in complete silence. Just as earlier in the commission, there was also objection to describing papal authority as "ordinary and immediate." Papal jurisdiction seemed, it was said, to be a "competing authority" that was superseding the likewise "ordinary and immediate" authority of the bishops. Yet the authority of the bishops was likewise of divine right and, as such, had to be respected by the pope. There were, therefore, demands for stating the secondary character of an immediate intervention of the pope in the dioceses; he should intervene only if required to do so for some need of the churches or for their benefit. It was felt, in addition, that it should be stated that the bishops have been appointed by God as shepherds of their churches and that they are not vicars of the pope. Thus the bishops made it unambiguously clear that in their view not only the primacy of the pope, but also the authority of the bishops, belongs to the God-given constitution of the church.

In addition, some bishops objected to having the primacy in the church of Christ described after the manner of the stern rule of secular princes. This made the primacy appear more as a hard yoke than as a gift from a loving God. Finally, there was objection to the pope being described as the "source of unity" of the church; the source of the church's unity is Christ alone, and the pope is only its "visible foundation." All in all, it is clear that the bishops at Vatican I affirmed papal primacy of jurisdiction, but that its definition as absolute sovereignty met with opposition.

The draft submissions of the council fathers were discussed by the competent commission, known as the Deputation on the Faith. The members stressed the point that the description of papal authority as ordinary, immediate, and episcopal could not, and was not intended, in any way to deny or weaken the authority of the bishops. To make this point clear, the following citation from Pope Gregory the Great was introduced into the text: "My honor is the honor of the whole Church. My honor is the firm strength of my brothers. I am truly honored when due honor is paid to each and every one."[21] These were the words with which Gregory the Great, in his own day, declined the title of "ecumenical patriarch pope." In the text of Vatican I, however, the pope is indeed described as "universal shepherd," while the bishops are called "particular shepherds." In addition, the pope is described as "supreme shepherd." No notice was taken of the bishops' call for mention of the fact that the college of bishops likewise possesses a supreme authority, although neither was this fact denied. We can thus see, once again, that the inherent authority of the bishops was expressly affirmed, especially in relation to their own dioceses, but the subject of their collegial co-responsibility for the universal church was not taken up by the deputation. The debate on the new text, now known as the First Constitution on the Church of Christ, began in May 1870. This text would eventually become the definitive constitution *Pastor Aeternus*. It no longer contained a complete teaching on the church but only the teaching of the council on the papacy. Four chapters treat of the establishment of the primacy, its perpetuity, its power and nature, and, finally, the infallible teaching office, or magisterium, of the Roman Pontiff.

The debate in the council confirmed the impression already given by the initial statements of the council fathers. All affirmed the pope's primacy of jurisdiction, but many sharply criticized its interpretation as absolute sovereignty. The church, they said, is not an absolute monarchy.[22] The respected German Bishop Wilhelm Emmanuel Ketteler explained: The authority of the pope is indeed the holiest, but not the sole authority in the church; the text constantly and at every point tends to define the pope's authority in extreme terms; the impression is thus given that the rights of the bishops are being denied and that the pope is being assigned a dominion (*dominium*) that belongs to Christ alone.[23]

Other council fathers objected that while the text gives assurances that the primacy affirms and defends the rights of the

---

21. M 53, 246 C; cf. ND 827.
22. M 52, 72 B, 1096 C.
23. M 52, 208 D–209 A.

bishops, these rights were nowhere listed.[24] Also passed over in silence were the limitations on the exercise of primacy and the existence of intermediate authorities in the church.[25] Another focus of attention in the debate was once again the description of papal jurisdiction as an ordinary, immediate, and episcopal authority.

The objection was frequently raised during the debate that the authority of the bishops was being limited to their individual dioceses. Some bishops reminded the fathers that the bishops, together with the pope, have a collegial responsibility for the universal church, just as at councils they have been legislators and teachers of the church.[26] This was denied by two bishops who claimed that this collegial responsibility was purely spiritual in nature and in no sense juridical.[27]

The response of the Deputation on the Faith to the criticisms and suggestions of the council fathers is of particular importance. This text constitutes an official commentary on the conciliar decree and is, therefore, an important help to its interpretation.

The spokesman for the deputation stated that the church is not to be understood as an absolute monarchy, for the pope is bound by divine and natural law and, therefore, cannot abolish the episcopate or its rights. But anyone claiming the authority of the pope can be limited by a human authority that is equal or superior to it is in error.[28] Here we can see the controlling purpose: to emphasize the autonomy of primacy of jurisdiction and to ensure its independence. But there is no denial of the rights of the episcopate, which limit the exercise of the primacy in virtue of divine law.

The spokesman for the deputation then responded to the fear that the pope is an absolute monarch at least in the sense that he does not have to observe the laws of the church. He declared that the pope would not annul "all canonical decisions enacted with wisdom and piety by the Apostles and the church." His rea-

---

24. M 52, 311 B.
25. M 52, 592 A, 682 B.
26. M 52, 282 BC; 310 AB; 393f.; 475 AC; 620 D.
27. M 52, 118f.; 582 AB.
28. M 52, 1114 D–1115 A.

son was that "moral theology teaches that the legislator is subject
to his own laws, if not by coercive power, at least in the manner of a directive." He added that precepts that are unjust and
harmful do not require obedience, except for the sake of avoiding
scandal.[29] Here again we see the effort of the Deputation on the
Faith to avoid letting the exercise of the primacy appear despotic.
This exercise is subject to the same moral obligations that bind
any other authority and must be directed to the welfare of the
church. The only thing being rejected is a limitation by any other
authority. The question of an effective check was left open, and
this silence allowed the maximalist interpreters to claim that the
pope is under obligation only to God and his own conscience.
However, the deputation did not say this.

The spokesman for the deputation also made an effort to clarify the meaning of the words "ordinary" and "immediate." The
term "ordinary" is used in the canonical sense to mean power
which is not delegated but belongs to the pope properly in virtue
of his office. He exercises this power in his own name and not
in the name of another. This explanation countered the bishops'
fear that "ordinary" meant the daily and continuous exercise of
papal authority in individual dioceses. The term "immediate"
means that the pope can exercise his authority directly without having to go through any intermediary, for example, the
permission of the local bishop.[30]

The spokesman for the deputation then went on to the controversial description of the pope's authority as "episcopal." He
explained that the pope has the same pastoral authority in the
entire church as the bishop has in his own diocese. Episcopal
authority has its source in the sacrament of episcopal consecration, so that both pope and bishops share in the same reality. But
there is a difference: "Episcopal authority in the pope is supreme
and independent; in the bishops it is immediate and ordinary but
dependent."[31]

---

29. M 52, 1109 A.
30. M 52, 1105 AB.
31. M 52, 1115 AB.

These explanations were doubtless capable of allaying some misgivings of the council fathers. But they passed over the fact that, by the laws he lays down, the pope intervenes in the life of the dioceses. As Bishop Maret and others had claimed, this fact suggested that the bishops should have a share in the lawmaking. The deputation also overlooked the fact that the episcopal character of papal authority makes the pope a member of the episcopal college. The distinction between "supreme and independent" and "dependent" places a one-sided emphasis on the position of the pope as head of the episcopal college, but does not explicitly tackle the subject of his membership in the college. Thus the explanations put no obstacle in the way of a papal centralization, just as some bishops feared.

Finally, the spokesman for the deputation responded to two requests, one of which had to do with the collegial co-responsibility of the bishops, while the other sought a participation of the bishops in the government of the universal church.[32] The requests were rejected on the grounds that, in the present context, the only issue was the full and immediate authority of the pope over the bishops. The council had no intention of resolving the controversial question of whether the jurisdiction of the bishops came directly from Christ or directly from the pope. On the other hand, there was no disagreement with the truth that the bishops, in union with their head, possessed supreme and full ecclesial authority over all the faithful, whether the bishops were scattered throughout the world or were assembled in an ecumenical council.[33]

This response of the Deputation on the Faith deserves special attention. On the one hand, no mention at all was made of the collegial collaboration of the bishops in the government of the universal church. The anti-Gallican thrust of the council was doubtless manifesting itself in this omission. Every suggestion along the lines requested was suspect of seeking a participation of the bishops in the jurisdictional primacy of the pope, as under-

---

32. M 52, 620f.; 1092 BC.
33. M 52, 1108 D–1110 C.

stood either in Gallicanism, which demanded the consent of the
bishops as a necessary condition for the validity of papal decisions, or by Maret, who proposed a sharing of papal sovereignty
in the passing of laws.

On the other hand (and this is surprising in view of the
customary interpretation of Vatican I), we see how clearly the
deputation asserted the authority of the college of bishops, and
this not merely when the bishops were meeting in council. The
spokesman repeated several times that supreme and full governmental authority has two forms. It exists in the bishops, together
with the pope: In the case of a council the bishops represent the
church; outside of a council they are the church. And this authority exists in the pope as head, even independently of his joint
actions with the other bishops. For the promises of Christ are
addressed both to all the apostles together with Peter, and to
Peter alone.

The spokesman then went into the problem raised by this
unique structure of government. The fact that supreme authority
exists in two forms does not lead to any dualism in the church.
On the contrary, both forms can peacefully coexist, as long as the
pope is not separated from the episcopate and the two forms are
not regarded as distinct and separated from each other.

Another point of great interest is the manner in which the deputation describes conciliarism and Gallicanism. According to its
spokesman, those who make the pope subject to the judgment of
the episcopate, or of a council, divide pope from episcopate as
though there were two different supreme authorities. Only then
can a conflict arise. Those who make such a division fail to understand that, apart from its head, the episcopate has no full and
supreme governmental authority; they also fail to understand the
primacy of the pope.[34]

The silence of the deputation on the collegial co-responsibility
of the bishops in the government of the universal church becomes
intelligible in light of these often overlooked utterances of the
Deputation on the Faith. The silence does not signify any rejec-

---

34. M 52, 1109 B–1110 B.

tion of this doctrine; in fact, it signifies the exact opposite. The deputation regarded the doctrine of the supreme and full authority of the college of bishops as a perfectly obvious integral part of the ecclesiastical and theological tradition. The truth that was controversial, and therefore needed to be defined, was the likewise supreme and full jurisdictional authority which the pope possesses independently of the active collaboration of the bishops. For this reason, the texts on primacy of jurisdiction had to set forth the proper origin and authority of this primacy, without introducing any formulas that could be misinterpreted along Gallican lines.

Of course, this unilateral emphasis on the primacy of jurisdiction was also motivated by the anti-Gallican and ultramontane attitude of the majority of the bishops. However, it would be an error to infer from this one-sidedness and from the silence of the council on the collegial co-responsibility of the bishops that the council intended to define the absolute sovereignty of the pope in the way understood by Cappellari and de Maistre.[35] A further confirmation of this interpretation of the conciliar decree is to be found in another text of the First Vatican Council. I am referring to the draft of the Second Constitution on the Church, which could not be further discussed and decided upon due to the premature suspension of the council. The text was the work of Joseph Kleutgen, S.J., a theologian at the council. It contains a chapter on the hierarchy of the church, in which the author explains the doctrine of the participation of the bishops in the supreme governmental and teaching authority over the entire church, as well as the doctrine of the authority of councils.[36] In his commentary Kleutgen explains that supreme and full authority exists in two subjects: in the body of bishops united with the pope and in the pope alone. This teaching, he says, is indeed difficult, but it is by no means new and is universally held.[37] In fact,

---

35. See Giuseppe Alberigo, *Lo sviluppo della dottrina sui poteri nella chiesa universale: Momenti essenziali tra il XVI e il XIX secolo* (Rome: Herder, 1964), 431–45.

36. M 53, 310 BC.

37. M 53, 321 BC.

Kleutgen considered the doctrine of the supreme authority of the college of bishops to be so certain that he describes it as a "most certain doctrine of the faith" (*fidei dogma certissimum*).[38]

It is obvious in this Second Constitution on the Church, that Kleutgen and the Deputation on the Faith intended to take into account the criticisms of those council fathers who had complained that in the first constitution no mention was made either of the rights of the bishops or of their collegial co-responsibility for the universal church. When the deputation was rejecting the requests of the bishops on those points, they were mindful of the fact that these concerns would be taken up in the Second Constitution on the Church.

The Definition of the Primacy of Jurisdiction

We have seen that the criticisms of the council fathers led to changes in the formulations of the primacy of jurisdiction: from absolute papal monarchy of the first drafts to a definition of primacy in the final draft that was indeed one-sided, but did remain open to the collegial dimension of the supreme governmental authority. On July 18, 1870, the council voted to accept the definitive version of the dogmatic constitution *Pastor Aeternus* on the church of Christ.

The third chapter of the constitution treats of "the power and nature of the primacy of the Roman Pontiff" (ND 825–29). The doctrine set forth in this chapter is summed up in the canon that follows it:

> And so, if anyone says that the Roman Pontiff has only the office of inspection and direction, but not the full and supreme power of jurisdiction over the whole Church, not only in matters that pertain to faith and morals, but also in matters that pertain to the discipline and government of the Church throughout the whole world; or if anyone says that he has only a more important part and not the complete fulness of this supreme power; or if anyone says that this power is not ordinary and immediate either over each and every

---

38. M 53, 322 B.

Church or over each and every shepherd and faithful, *anathema sit.* (ND 830)

Here and in the corresponding chapter, the primacy of jurisdiction of the pope is defined as a supreme and full, universal, ordinary, immediate, and truly episcopal power of ruling, judging, and teaching in the church with the consequent obligation of obedience.

Anyone relying exclusively on this definition for the interpretation of Vatican I can very easily come to the conclusion that the council made a dogma of the absolute sovereignty and monarchy of the pope. However, an examination of the conciliar debates has shown that this was not the council's intention. Is it possible to find evidence of this even in the text of the constitution itself? Yes, it is.

The introduction, for example, speaks of the mission of all the apostles to be shepherds and teachers in the church (ND 818). It also speaks of the unity of the episcopate and the communion of believers, which Peter has been called to preserve. In these statements the existence of the college of bishops is at least hinted at.

But the most important point for the interpretation of Vatican I is the fact that the council repeatedly appeals to the ancient and universal tradition of the church: "according to the ancient and constant belief of the universal church" (ND 818); "relying on the clear testimony of the Holy Scriptures and following the express and definite decrees of our predecessors, the Roman Pontiffs, and of the general Councils" (ND 825); "the perpetual practice of the Church . . . and the ecumenical Councils, especially those in which the Western and Eastern Churches were united in faith and love" (ND 831). Even though the continuity, here asserted, with the ancient tradition is dubious, as we have seen, the council intended, in any case, to locate its definition within the framework and under the standard of the universal tradition, expressly including even the tradition of the first millennium. This intention also found expression in the fact that the Deputation on the Faith explicitly affirmed the doctrine of the full and supreme authority of the college of bishops and of councils. Thus the co-existence of primacy and episcopate as experienced and taught in earlier centuries remains valid and forms a critical corrective to the one-sidedness of the definition issued by Vatican I. The Council thereby implicitly acknowledged a plurality of possible concrete forms of primacy in the past and in the future.

In response to the criticisms of the council fathers, the third chapter on primacy included an assurance that papal primacy was not meant to detract from the jurisdiction of the bishops in their dioceses. The bishops are described as "true shepherds" of their dioceses:

> This power of the Supreme Pontiff is far from standing in the way of the power of ordinary and immediate episcopal jurisdiction by which the bishops who, under appointment of the Holy Spirit (cf. Acts 20:28), succeeded in the place of the apostles, feed and rule individually, as true shepherds, the particular flock assigned to them. Rather this latter power is asserted, confirmed and vindicated by this same supreme and universal shepherd, as in the words of St. Gregory the Great: "My honor is the honor of the whole Church. My honor is the firm strength of my brothers. I am truly honored when due honor is paid to each and every one." (ND 827)

However, valuable and important as these indications are, the fact remains that the constitution defined the primacy of jurisdiction in a consciously one-sided way. As a conciliar theologian, Apollinaris Maier, made emphatically clear, the one-sided emphasis on the supreme power of the pope was meant to be understood positively and affirmatively, not exclusively.[39] But because the council avoided discussing and formulating the criteria for an appropriate exercise of the primacy, an exercise that would respect the rights of the bishops and the local churches, this made it possible for the text to be given subsequently a maximalist interpretation. It takes an examination of the other records of the council to make it clear that the council did not intend to define primacy as absolute sovereignty of the pope.

It was, therefore, not without some basis that in a circular letter to the European governments in 1872 Bismarck, the Ger-

---

39. M 52, 11 CD.

man chancellor, leveled the accusation that the council had made the pope sovereign and absolute monarch of the church and had made bishops into mere executive organs of the pope, and that the latter were thus degraded to the status of mere officials. The response which the German bishops made to this accusation in the Collective Declaration of 1875 became an important document for the interpretation of Vatican I. For, in an apostolic brief of March 4, 1875,[40] and in a consistorial allocution of March 15, 1875, Pope Pius IX gave approval to this declaration in an unusually solemn form. The declaration of the German bishops says:

> It is in virtue of the same divine institution upon which the papacy rests that the episcopate also exists. It, too, has its rights and duties, because of the ordinance of God himself, and the Pope has neither the right nor the power to change them. Thus it is a complete misunderstanding of the Vatican decrees to believe that because of them "episcopal jurisdiction has been absorbed into the papal," that the Pope has "in principle taken the place of each individual bishop," that the bishops are now "no more than tools of the Pope, his officials, without responsibility of their own." (ND 841)

The language of this document is doubtless clearer than that of the constitution *Pastor Aeternus* itself. With papal approval, it explicitly rejects the maximalizing ultramontane interpretation of Vatican I, namely, that "as a result of these [the decrees of the Vatican Council] the pope has become an absolute sovereign."[41] The formulations in this document certainly do not support a Vatican centralization.[42] The fact that after Vatican I the maximalist interpretation came to prevail, and a Vatican centralization resulted, is due only partially to the one-sided emphasis on the primacy of jurisdiction in the constitution *Pastor Aeternus*. This fact was due much more to the isolation and defensive attitude of Catholicism in many countries and in modern society. This ecclesiastical centralization was a matter of strategy more than of

---

40. DS 3117.
41. DS 3114.
42. See Umberto Betti, *La costituzione dommatica "Pastor Aeternus" del Concilio Vaticano I* (Rome: Antonianum, 1961), 624f.; Jean-Pierre Torrell, *La théologie de l'episcopat au premier concile du Vatican* (Paris: Cerf, 1961).

theology. As a strategy it was remarkably successful, but it was never theologically compelling. The presentation of it as theologically compelling, as in the maximalist interpretation, was rather a part of the strategy.

This judgment is confirmed by the analyses I have given in the second and third chapters of this book. For this one-sided development and conception of papal primacy to become possible, and for a Vatican centralization to take form, it took both the struggle of the medieval popes (and later popes) for the independence of the church, as well as the traumatic quest of security at the time of Vatican I. Ultramontanism, which was not so much a theology as it was a strategy and ideology for the strengthening of the primacy, arose because the papacy showed itself capable of resisting pressure from the political interests of princes and states and of being a point of reference for unsettled Catholics. The ultramontane treatment of the pope as an absolute monarch and sovereign was an ideological action because it narrowed the theological tradition in the service of the ultramontane strategy. The council fathers of Vatican I were pressured and influenced by ultramontane interests and strategies. Against this historical background, it is especially remarkable that the council resisted the ideological pressure and did not betray the original ecclesiastical and theological tradition regarding the episcopal and collegial constitution of the church. It neither declared, nor intended to declare, the pope absolute sovereign and monarch.

Thus the analysis of Vatican I, of its course and decisions, yields this result: that Vatican centralization cannot appeal to Vatican I for its theological justification. That council taught the proper origin and particular authority of papal primacy of jurisdiction by invoking the special mission of Peter, but it did not deny the proper origin, and equally supreme authority, of the college of bishops. More than that, Vatican I declared that primacy is obliged to assert, confirm, and vindicate the authority of the bishops in their dioceses. The council did not determine the scope of the primatial rights of the pope, which have changed in the course of history. The council did not make its own the claim that the jurisdiction of the bishops comes directly from the pope (this, in Bishop Maret's view, was the central point of the "absolutist school"). Finally, the council let it be understood that it did not intend any break with the tradition of the first millennium and the tradition of the churches of the East.

This result yields two insights that are important for a theological assessment of Vatican I. First, the council and its decrees leave open the possibility that the Petrine office may take various forms and that primacy may be exercised in a variety of ways — a variety that has actually been displayed in the tradition and history of the church. The council simply asserted that primacy, as the pope was exercising it at that time and as, in the council's judgment, he was bound to exercise it in the current situation for the greatest good of the church, is a legitimate concrete form of that Petrine office which goes back to Peter and his mission.

Second, Vatican I is open, and not an obstacle, to the ecclesiology of communion which Vatican II tried to formulate, and in which it intended to establish ties with the tradition of the still undivided church of the first millennium. As the statements of the Deputation on the Faith attest, the theologically educated fathers of Vatican I were aware of this: that the concrete form of interplay of papal and episcopal authority in individual dioceses was a question which the council could not, and did not, intend to answer in the constitution. Nor did *Pastor Aeternus* deal with how the collaborative exercise of the governmental authority of primate and college of bishops would function in the setting of the universal church.

CHAPTER FIVE

Vatican I and the Infallibility
of the Papal Teaching Office

Nice

The Pyrrhic Victory of the Maximalist Interpretation
of the Infallibility Dogma

The doctrine of Vatican I on the infallible magisterium of the
pope is today a dogma of the Catholic Church that produces
smiles rather than controversy. But at the time of Vatican I and
during the council itself it was the number one topic. At the council it split the bishops into a minority that advised against the
definition of papal infallibility and a majority that wanted infallibility defined. Among Catholics, the definition was the principal
desire of the ultramontanists. Among the general public and in
the press this doctrine seemed proof that the Catholic Church
was stuck fast in the Middle Ages.

Today, according to polls, the dogma of Vatican I on infallibility is not accepted even by the majority of Catholics in many
countries. One of the main reasons why this dogma is so unper-
suasive is the maximalist interpretation that has been given to it.
As in the case of the dogma of the primacy of jurisdiction, here
too it was Catholic catechesis itself that saw to the spread of this
maximalist interpretation. It was only because this scarcely credible understanding of the dogma of infallibility was so widespread
that, in 1970, with his book *Infallible? An Inquiry*, Hans Küng
was able to unleash a theological debate which exceeded in in-
tensity all other discussions after Vatican II.[1] His presumption —

1. Hans Küng, *Infallible? An Inquiry* (New York: Doubleday, 1971).

76

that Vatican I defined an untenable maximalist view of infallibility — was rejected by the majority of Catholic theologians and
was one of the reasons why Küng was removed from the Catholic
department of theology at Tübingen.[2] In any case, the discussion
led to a series of historical studies of the dogma of infallibility.
It was chiefly the studies of Ulrich Horst and Klaus Schatz that
showed Küng's thesis to be untenable.[3]

Nonetheless, the maximalist interpretation of the dogma of
infallibility persists even today. It seems to find confirmation in
a phenomenon described as "sweeping infallibility" or "galloping infallibility." What is meant is the tendency to attach to the
doctrinal utterances of the pope or the Roman Curia an extraor-
dinarily far-reaching claim to authority and obedience. Whereas
Vatican I distinguished clearly between infallible dogmatic decisions and noninfallible utterances of the pope, this distinction has
recently been in danger of being blurred. The intended result is to
ensure greater attention to Vatican doctrinal statements.

It is doubtful, however, that this strategy is producing the de-
sired result. Recent inquiry shows that the contrary effect is being
produced and that there has been an erosion of ecclesiastical, and
especially Vatican, authority. This is regrettable, given the lack of
direction in contemporary society. Also regrettable is the effect of
this strategy on ecumenical dialogue. Since the strategy encourages the maximalist interpretation of the infallibility dogma and
feeds the suspicion that in the Catholic Church doctrinal centralization follows necessarily from Vatican I, that council seems to

---

2. See John J. Kirvan, ed., *The Infallibility Debate* (New York: Paulist, 1971);
NCCB Committee on Doctrine, *The Küng Dossier* (Washington, D.C.: USCC,
1980); Terry J. Tekippe, ed., *Papal Infallibility: An Application of Lonergan's
Theological Method* (Washington: University Press of America, 1983).

3. Ulrich Horst, *Unfehlbarkeit und Geschichte: Studien zur Unfehlbarkeitsdiskussion von Melchior Cano bis zum 1. Vatikanischen Konzil* (Mainz:
Grünewald, 1982); Klaus Schatz, *Kirchenbild und päpstliche Unfehlbarkeit bei den
deutschsprachigen Minoritätsbischöfen auf dem I. Vatikanum* (Rome: Gregoriana,
1975); Klaus Schatz, *Vaticanum I, 1869–1870,* 3 vols. (Paderborn: Schöningh,
1992–94); see also Margaret O'Gara, *Triumph in Defeat: Infallibility, Vatican I,
and the French Minority Bishops* (Washington, D.C.: Catholic University of America Press, 1988).

be an insuperable obstacle to ecumenism. In what follows I shall
show that this is not the case.

Infallibility as an Element in Sovereignty

In his circular letter to the European governments in 1872, Bismarck, the German chancellor, voiced the objection that as a
result of the council's decrees the pope "had become an absolute
monarch and even, because of his infallibility, completely absolute, more so than any other absolute monarch in the world."[4]
However, this objection did not reflect the actual teaching of Vatican I. Bismarck was correct, however, concerning the goal which
the ultramontane movement was seeking in its conception of
papal infallibility. In the eyes of this movement, infallibility was
an element in absolute sovereignty, indeed an element without
which papal sovereignty would remain incomplete. Infallibility
would make the sovereignty of the pope superior even to the sovereignty of secular rulers and states and was intended, in this way,
to ensure his absolute independence.

Mauro Cappellari was the first to conceive of jurisdictional
primacy as sovereignty.[5] His view was that infallibility is an
element of papal sovereignty and a necessary property of the primacy of jurisdiction. According to him, "the gift of infallibility is
a privilege inseparable from the primacy."[6]

This same view appears even more in Joseph de Maistre. He
made not only papal sovereignty but also papal infallibility key
points in his program: "The more pope, the more sovereignty;
the more sovereignty, the more unity; the more unity, the more
authority, the more authority, the more faith."[7] De Maistre could
not conceive of sovereignty apart from infallibility.

---

4. DS 3114.
5. See Horst, *Unfehlbarkeit und Geschichte*, 96–120.
6. Mauro Cappellari, *Il trionfo della Santa Sede e della Chiesa contro gli assalti
de' novatori respinti e combattuti colle stesse loro armi* (Rome, 1799), 373.
7. Joseph de Maistre, *Lettres et opuscules inédits* (Lyon, 1851) 2:296.

> There can be no human society without a government, no govern-
> ment without sovereignty, no sovereignty without infallibility, and
> this last privilege is so absolutely necessary that one is compelled to
> postulate infallibility even in secular sovereignties (where it does not
> exist) if one is not to concede the ultimate dissolution of the social
> order.[8]

Here we see, completely undisguised, the strategic and ideological nature of the ultramontane conception of infallibility.
Infallibility is a necessary property of sovereign power because
the claim of infallibility is indispensable for effective rule. Ernest
Renan perceptively remarked that what de Maistre wanted was
not really an infallible pope but "a pope from whom there is
no appeal."[9] Jean Bodin and Thomas Hobbes claimed that being
a court of last appeal is the very heart of the idea of sovereignty. It was out of the same concern for efficient government
that Hobbes proposed his well-known principle: "Authority, not
truth, makes law" (*Auctoritas, non veritas, facit legem*).[10] The
difference is that his concern for efficiency and the impossibility
of appeal did not lead Hobbes to claim infallibility for governments; in contrast to de Maistre, he called for the complete
leaving out of consideration of the question of truth.

The issue for de Maistre and the other theoreticians of sovereignty was the question of who has the right to make final
decisions in the state or the church. The influence of Bodin and
Hobbes on de Maistre is unmistakable.[11] However, in dealing
with the church and the pope, de Maistre could not separate the
right of final decision from the claim to truth. For this reason, he
had to call for the infallibility of the pope as a necessary property
of his primacy of jurisdiction.

The influence exercised by de Maistre's ideas can be seen in
Félicité Lamennais, the other thinker who prepared the way for

---

8. Joseph de Maistre, *Du Pape* (Lyon, 1819; Geneva, 1966), 123.

9. Ernest Renan, *L'avenir de la science* (1848; Paris, 1890), 62 n. 31.

10. Thomas Hobbes, *Leviathan* (Amsterdam, 1670), 133.

11. See Richard A. Lebrun, *Throne and Altar: The Political and Religious
Thought of J. de Maistre* (Ottawa: University of Ottawa Press, 1965); J. H.
Franklin, *Jean Bodin and the Rise of Absolutist Theory* (Cambridge: Cambridge
University Press, 1973).

ultramontanism. In his review of de Maistre's *The Pope* Lamennais expressly agrees with its author: "We have seen that since the
church is a society it must possess a sovereign power or — this is
the same thing — an infallible authority."[12] Only later on, after
his disillusionment with the policies of Gregory XVI, did Lamennais adopt a more nuanced view of papal infallibility; he admitted
that, when defending the church and the papacy, he had, in the
heat of battle, been "a little too much a soldier."[13]

It is of interest to note the roundabout ways by which de
Maistre's ideas entered the church and theology.[14] In the 1820s
de Maistre and Lamennais repeatedly complained of the papacy's attitude of reserve. A Vatican censor faulted de Maistre
for confusing infallibility with the impossibility of appeal and for
speaking disparagingly of the authority of councils. According to
Lamennais, the reason for the caution shown by the papacy and
the theologians was that they relied too much on the testimonies
of tradition instead of being guided by reason. And, in fact, in addition to Lamennais, it was primarily philosophers and political
thinkers who agreed with de Maistre's ideas. The idea of an infallible authority was picked up by, among others, Claude Henri
de Saint-Simon, Auguste Comte, Juan F. Donoso Cortés, Jaime L.
Balmes, and the German Romantics.

Nonetheless, it was, above all, the writings of Lamennais, and
later of his disciples, that paved the way for the idea that primacy
and infallibility are necessarily interconnected. In the 1840s this
idea gained acceptance in France. In 1857 a journalist in Rome
reported that here, too, de Maistre's new system had replaced
the ultramontanism of the sixteenth century and the theology of
Cardinal Bellarmine. On the other hand, there were still many
theologians in the schools of theology who stayed with proven
theological methods and relied on the testimonies of tradition.

---

12. Félicité de la Mennais, *Oeuvres complètes* (Paris 1836–37; Frankfurt 1967),
8:117.

13. Ibid., 10:xvi; see Hermann J. Pottmeyer, *Unfehlbarkeit und Souveränität:
Die päpstliche Unfehlbarkeit im System der ultramontanen Ekklesiologie des 19.
Jahrhunderts* (Mainz: Grünewald, 1975), 73–88.

14. See Pottmeyer, *Unfehlbarkeit*, 89–345.

Many of them, their numbers growing, supported the doctrine of papal infallibility, but they also maintained the traditional doctrine: the infallibility of councils, of the college of bishops, and of the consensus of the church on matters of faith.

De Maistre's idea of an unconditional infallibility was successful because it promised security and certainty in an age in which previously fixed arrangements and certainties were breaking down. People hoped that the restoration of the principle of authority would lead to a renewal of society and moral values. What people now needed, according to de Maistre, was not problems and discussions but dogmas.[15] In like manner, English journalist William G. Ward, editor of the *Dublin Review* and an active ultramontanist, expressed a wish that every morning at breakfast he might read in the *Times* the latest infallible declaration of the pope on controversial questions of the day.[16] Even though these were extreme views, the bishops who were starting out for the First Vatican Council felt the pressure of the expectation of many Catholics that the council would define papal infallibility in order to strengthen the papacy.

The Conciliar Debate: Three Views in Conflict

In order to answer the question whether Vatican I defined papal infallibility as understood by the extreme ultramontanists and according to the maximalist interpretation, it is not necessary to investigate everything that happened before, during, and after the council. There are numerous studies of that already. The only important thing is to note that three conceptions of papal infallibility were in a struggle to have it defined as they understood it.

The ultramontane position that followed de Maistre was represented at the council by a small group of extreme infallibilists. Their leaders were Archbishop Manning of Westminster and Bishop Senestrey of Regensburg. These two individuals were the

---

15. Joseph de Maistre, "Étude sur la souveraineté," in *Oeuvres complètes* (Lyon, 1884), 1:425.

16. See Roger Aubert, *Le pontificat de Pie IX* (Paris: Cerf, 1963), 302.

real strategists of the council when it came to the question of infallibility, and they enjoyed a good relationship with Pius IX. This group was opposed by a minority that numbered about 20 percent of the council fathers. These members were either critical of the definition of papal infallibility or rejected it altogether. They were agreed primarily in rejecting the extreme conception of infallibility, because they regarded it as incompatible with the testimonies of tradition. This group included chiefly bishops from Germany, Austria, and Hungary, from France, the United States, and the East. Finally, there was the majority, who presented no clear, distinguishing image, but they were inclined to accept some definition of papal infallibility. Since these bishops came out ever more clearly on the side of a definition as the council proceeded, the extreme infallibilists were usually reckoned as part of this majority. Within the majority there were a number of bishops who were open to the concerns of the minority and sought a solution on which all could agree, but they did not form a definite group. Of the council fathers from the United States, 21 could be counted among the minority, 10 among the infallibilists, and 6 for the mediating position.[17]

On March 6, 1870, the draft of the chapter on infallibility, which had been composed by council theologian Joseph Kleutgen, S.J., was distributed to the fathers.[18] The latter were asked to give their views on it in writing. In 139 statements 255 council fathers did so. Of the council fathers 83 expressed themselves against the definition. The extreme infallibilists among them wanted a stronger anti-Gallican emphasis.

The views of the bishops were then discussed by the Deputation on the Faith, which was composed of extreme infallibilists and members of the majority. The deputation decided to combine the chapters on papal primacy and papal infallibility into the First Constitution on the Church; the fourth chapter of this text contained the teaching on papal infallibility. This draft was

---

17. See Schatz, *Vaticanum I*, 2:23–55.
18. M 51, 701f.

distributed to the council fathers on May 9, 1870.[19] The general debate on the draft began on May 14.

The minority objected to the fact that the text took as its starting point a separate, absolute, and personal infallibility of the pope: separate because any papal decision would be made without the collaboration of the bishops; absolute, because it would not be subject to any ascertainable conditions; personal, because in the final analysis it would depend solely on the will of the pope. The minority suggested adopting, instead, the formula of St. Antoninus: The pope is not infallible when he acts as an individual and on his own initiative, but he is when he makes use of the advice and help of the entire church.[20]

This first debate already made it clear that not only the minority but also many bishops of the majority rejected the position of the extreme infallibilists as represented by de Maistre. The infallibility of the pope, they explained, is based not on an inspiration but on the promise made to Peter, which also ensures that the pope will use appropriate means to obtain certainty on the faith of the church and that he will hold fast to this. On the other hand, the council may not make the infallibility of the pope dependent on the collaboration of the bishops or other conditions.

However, the bishops of the majority did not offer only theological reasons for this position. They rejected the establishment of conditions primarily for another reason: There must be in the church an authority that can quickly and effectively issue a final decision that is valid without any reservations. If conditions are imposed, the discussion will never end as to whether or not the conditions have been met. This argument coincides, of course, with the concern of de Maistre and of the ultramontanist conception. The primary motive of the majority at the council was thus *strategic* and not *theological*. At the theological level, the concern of the minority that the pope be bound by the faith of the

---

19. M 52, 4–7.
20. See Horst, *Unfehlbarkeit und Geschichte*, 234.

church was not challenged by most bishops of the majority; on the contrary, it was explicitly affirmed.

Only the extreme infallibilists stated a theological argument against the minority position. They insisted that the church and its infallibility depend on the pope and his infallibility, and not the other way around. Therefore they rejected not only any conditions for the exercise of papal infallibility, but also any limitations on its scope.

This debate showed the reasons for the one-sided tendency of the infallibility dogma. What the minority wanted was not simply a statement that the pope must, in principle, hold fast to the faith of the church. Rather, there also needed to be some possibility of ascertaining whether, in issuing a doctrinal decision, the pope was, in fact, holding to the faith of the church. The best way to achieve this was through the collaboration and agreement of the episcopate. This demand of the minority was rejected for two reasons: by the extreme infallibilists because of their conception of infallibility as an element in the absolute sovereignty of the pope; and by most bishops of the majority because of the already mentioned strategy and because of their desire to strengthen the effectiveness of papal authority.

The issue, then, in the conflict between the extreme infallibilists and the minority was the acceptance or rejection of papal primacy conceived as absolute sovereignty. In the conflict between majority and minority, on the other hand, the issue was one of priorities. The minority gave priority to the truthfulness of the pope's witness to the common faith tradition of the church; the majority gave priority to the independence and efficacy of papal authority.

Thus it was the subject of papal infallibility that brought the real confrontation between the paradigm of the first millennium and that of the second. Still alive in the minority was the conviction of the first millennium that in determining the faith of the church the common witness of the college of bishops and the pope was more authoritative than that of the pope alone. On the level of witness, the absolute sovereignty of the pope was unthinkable to the minority, nor was the priority of the majority acceptable. Conversely, the majority feared that conciliarism and Gallicanism would not be overcome as long as the pope was dependent on the bishops in determining the faith of the church. In their view conciliarism and Gallicanism meant a weakening of the papacy and a crippling of the church. Their priority, therefore, was the strengthening of papal authority, so the church might be seen as an independent and self-determining subject and might act effectively. This was the priority and the paradigm of the second millennium.

However, it would be inaccurate to reduce the problem to the conflict between the paradigms of the first and second millennia, to the conflict between the priority of truthful witness and the priority of an effective power of jurisdiction. The problem which the council faced was the twofold nature of every dogmatic decree of the magisterium, whether the magisterium of a council or of a pope. Such a decree is both a testimony that ascertains and formulates the authentic faith of the church, and an act of the supreme power of jurisdiction, which commands acceptance of this decree and calls for the obedience of faith from all of the faithful. According to traditional teaching, pope and bishops in a council are both witnesses and judges. The same is true of the pope when he issues a dogmatic decree on his own. Because of the twofold nature of a dogmatic decree (witness that communicates the truth and ecclesiastical law that is an act of jurisdiction) the theologians and canonists of the nineteenth century disagreed on whether the hierarchical teaching office was to be assigned to the power of jurisdiction or was a separate power.[21]

Vatican I left this question open. In the early drafts infallibility was introduced as a necessary property of the papal power of jurisdiction; this corresponded to de Maistre's position. However, the final text says "that the supreme power of teaching is also included in this apostolic primacy which the Roman Pontiff...holds" (ND 831). This change from "power of jurisdiction" to "apostolic primacy" resulted from the objec-

---

21. See Pottmeyer, *Unfehlbarkeit*, 371–88.

tion of the minority that the teaching office is also to be seen as
authoritative witnessing.

In the dispute for and against papal infallibility, then, Vatican I
was not dealing only with a conflict between different conceptions, priorities, and paradigms. The council also faced the task
of doing justice to the complex nature of every dogmatic decision of the ecclesiastical magisterium. Only now, in the question
of papal infallibility, was the task seen with this degree of clarity. In the first millennium it did not yet emerge because at that
time a dogmatic decree was seen primarily as witness to a tradition that was to be preserved unchanged. Even in the case of
a council the question of the complex nature of a dogmatic decision did not arise with the same clarity. For in the work of a
council the jurisdictional act of legislating follows directly from
the joint determination of the faith tradition and thus from the
testimony of the bishops, and is the joint act of pope and bishops. In the case of a dogmatic decision of the pope by himself,
the immediate connection of these two components is no longer
self-evident. The question has to be asked therefore whether and
how the pope bases his decision on the testimony of the church
and the faith tradition. It was precisely with this question that the
minority confronted the majority. De Maistre and the extreme infallibilists ignored this question in their conception with its focus
on decision-making. This happened either because they replaced
infallibility with the impossibility of appeal or because of their
quasi-mystical exaltation of the papacy.

An example of this exaltation may be seen in an infallibilist
bishop who asserted in the council hall that "the pope is, so to
speak, an incarnation of the supernatural order...and therefore
the nations may behold in the teaching pope the supernatural
order and Christ within it, who therefore in all things and for
all is in the pope and with the pope and through the pope."[22]

The minority, however, did not simply raise the question of
the nature of a papal doctrinal decision as a witness to the com-

---

22. M 52, 767 A.

mon faith. They also insisted that the bishops must, in one way or another, share in the determination of the truth. The minority repeatedly made the collegial co-responsibility of the bishops for the universal church a central theme in the discussion of the primacy of jurisdiction. Now, in the question of papal infallibility, their theological concern was the role of the bishops as official witnesses and teachers of the faith to their churches and, at the same time, the bishop's responsibility for the common faith of the universal church. Thus the minority brought out their understanding of the church in their criticism of a one-sided definition of papal infallibility. In keeping with the tradition of the first millennium, the bishops of the minority understood that the church is a communion of churches and a communion of witnesses to the common faith. An aspect of this church, in their view, was also the organic union of pope and bishops as official witnesses and teachers of the common faith.

The Struggle for an Agreement: Strategy vs. Theology

Two observations are important for a correct interpretation of Vatican I and its dogma of infallibility. First, the conception of the church as a communion was also present in the debate on papal infallibility. Second, while the theological concerns of this concept were admittedly perceived and affirmed to only a limited degree by many and influential members of the majority, neither were these concerns rejected. This fact was confirmed several times in the further course of the conciliar debate.

The first confirmation of that observation was the decision of the Deputation on the Faith to introduce into the chapter on papal infallibility a text that represented an important concession to the minority. The purpose of the text was to make it clear that the pope does not exercise his office as teacher of the church except in union and unity with the church; therefore explicit mention was to be made of consulting scripture, tradition, and synods or councils.[23] This text would later become a section of chapter 4 of the constitution *Pastor Aeternus* and is very important for the interpretation of the dogma of infallibility.

A second confirmation was provided by an incident that doubtless was the high point of the debate on infallibility. The second day of the special debate on chapter 4 was June 15, 1870. Cardinal Guidi, archbishop of Bologna and a member of the Dominican order, signed up to speak.[24] He was one of the majority bishops who showed an openness to the theological concerns of the minority. The purpose of his effort was to bring about a greater attention to these concerns in the text of the council.

Guidi could rely on a long theological tradition of his order which made a strict distinction between the pope's power of jurisdiction and his teaching office. According to Guidi, the pope's power of jurisdiction is a constant and complete power in the exercise of which he is completely independent of the consent or advice of the bishops. Insofar as a dogmatic decree of a pope is an act of his power of jurisdiction, he decides independently whether, when, and how he acts. However, Guidi asserted that insofar as a dogmatic decree defines the faith of the church and is to be a witness to the common faith, the pope is indeed dependent on the advice and collaboration of the bishops. It is with their help that he must ascertain what the "sense of the faith" of the entire church is, what the tradition of the individual churches is, and what has been believed everywhere, always, and by all in the question to be decided. For the divine assistance that preserves the pope from error in a definition of the faith is not a habitual quality that modifies the intellect of the pope and interiorly determines it. It is, instead, a transient, actual help that has to do with the act and not the person. It is not the pope, but his definition, that is infallible. From all these considerations Guidi concluded that it is the duty of the pope to consult with the bish-

---

23. M 53, 258 B.
24. See Horst, *Unfehlbarkeit und Geschichte*, 164–213; Schatz, *Vaticanum I,* 3:99–109.

ops. Otherwise, he said, we must assume that a new and special revelation is given to the pope.[25]

Cardinal Guidi's address caused a sensation. It was not hailed by the minority alone. Members of the majority, too, saw in his proposals a bridge leading to an agreement between minority and majority. Guidi's address represented a respected tradition that was older than the idea of an absolute infallibility. Moreover, it did justice to the twofold nature of a dogmatic definition, because it took into account equally the two aspects of a definition as witness and as an act of jurisdiction. Guidi thus provided the opportunity for a coalition of the minority and the receptive section of the majority.

Unfortunately, Pius IX, who at this time wanted no more compromising with the minority, gave this attempt at an agreement no chance of succeeding. On that very same day he summoned Cardinal Guidi and, in a state of great agitation, reproached him severely. It was on this occasion that the pope uttered the famous words: "I am the tradition!"

How did the Deputation on the Faith react to Guidi's address? In view of its strong effect, the deputation thought a special statement necessary. This clearly betrayed the uncertainty which Guidi's address had stirred in those bishops of the majority who were inclined to the extreme infallibilist position. The spokesman for the deputation sharply rejected Guidi's proposals, but the reasons he gave sounded empty and did not come to grips with Guidi's real theological argument.[26]

The main reason for the rejection must be noted. In the opinion of the deputation, those who, like Guidi, spoke of an inherent appropriateness or inherent necessity of consultation and episcopal collaboration were endangering the effectiveness of papal authority, because such consultation and cooperation could possibly be misunderstood as a legal condition for the validity of papal decisions. Past experience showed, according to the spokesman, that if the duty of consultation were mentioned in the

---

25. M 52, 741–48.
26. M 52, 760 C–767 C.

definition, it would once again lead to endless discussions of the
validity of papal decisions. Here is confirmation, once again, that
the real reason for rejecting Guidi's proposals and the concerns
of the minority was strategic and not theological.

This last point became even clearer when the spokesman went
on to protest that the pope had a moral obligation, before any
definition, to inform himself about the faith of the church from
scripture and tradition and this with the help of the bishops or
in some other way. This, he said, is normal procedure (*factum
ordinarium*).[27] The pope was obliged to exercise diligent care in
this matter, since this is the necessary (*necessario*) means of ascertaining truth.[28] However, the spokesman suggested that the moral
obligation does not belong in the definition itself. Moreover, the
promise of divine assistance ensures that the pope will not act
capriciously.

Finally, there is a further argument which, strangely enough,
is based on the collegial structure of the teaching office. A mention of the cooperation of the episcopate is unnecessary, the
spokesman said, even from the viewpoint of the bishops. For,
since the entire teaching church, made up of the pope and the
bishops, is infallible, the bishops knew that a separation of pope
from bishops is impossible and therefore that the bishops would
always follow the pope.[29] Even though the role of the bishops
appears here only in a reduced form, the argument nonetheless
shows that the council remained aware of the collegial structure
of the ecclesiastical teaching office.

In any case, the answer of the spokesman for the Deputation
on the Faith showed how close to each other Guidi's proposals and the position of the majority were and how suited these
proposals were for achieving an agreement. Guidi, too, emphasized the juridical independence of the pope and did not intend
the pope's obligation to consult and the bishops' cooperation to
be understood as a juridical condition for the validity of papal
definitions. What separated the majority and Guidi was that the

27. M 52, 763 D.
28. M 52, 764 D.
29. M 52, 765 C.

latter thought in theological terms, the former in strategic terms. The majority's primary concern was to condemn Gallicanism and strengthen the effectiveness of papal authority. It could not deny the weightiness of Guidi's theological concerns.

For this reason, the deputation was, in fact, admitting the practical consequences that followed from the complex nature of a dogmatic definition with its essential interconnection of witness and jurisdiction. When the spokesman described diligent and careful consultation by the pope as materially and morally necessary and as normal procedure, this was precisely what Guidi and the minority wanted. The difference was that they wanted this normal procedure and obligation to be mentioned even in the definition as the expression of the pope's commitment to the church. But this specific item was rejected by the deputation again for strategic reasons. Its spokesman did, however, promise that consultation would be mentioned in the chapter as normal procedure, as the deputation had already decided.

Despite being rejected, Guidi's address had caused the deputation to study the concerns of the minority to a greater extent than before and, where it thought possible, to take them into account.

Another conspicuous effort at agreement, this time from the minority, was that of Bishop Ketteler; his thinking was along the same line as Guidi's.[30] He proposed four principles that would avoid the definition of a personal, separate, and absolute infallibility. First, the pope is dependent on human means, the foremost of which is the judgment of the bishops; whether and how the pope lets the bishops play a part depends on circumstances. Second, divine providence ensures that these means are always used, so that the definition will be a testimony to the common faith; therefore papal definitions are not to be called into doubt later on. Third, scripture and tradition are the sources of every dogmatic definition. Fourth, the object of an infallible definition can only be a revealed truth and whatever is inseparably connected with it.

After Guidi's address, that of Ketteler showed, once again,

---

30. M 52, 890–99.

how close to each other were the members of minority and
majority who were prepared to enter into an agreement. A
counteraddress was delivered by French Bishop Charles E. Freppel.[31] Although Ketteler's second principle explicitly excluded any
misunderstanding of a Gallican kind, Freppel insisted that, because of the danger of such a misunderstanding, the human
means should not be mentioned in the definition itself. The point
that became clear here once again also emerged in the remainder
of the special debate: What divided minority and majority (except
for the extreme infallibilists) was not theological considerations
but the strategic reasons of the majority.

Only one bishop claimed that a clear distinction should be
made between *ex cathedra* decisions and other magisterial utterances of the pope. Without this distinction, he said, defenders of
excessive views of papal infallibility could, in the long run, cause
greater problems than their opponents did; it is out of the question that everything the popes have taught should be regarded as
dogma.[32]

As a matter of fact, in its subsequent assessment of the debate,
the deputation decided on a formula that would distinguish between an *ex cathedra* decision and other magisterial utterances
of the pope. In addition, it adopted the suggestion of Guidi and
others for the title of the chapter. Instead of "The Infallibility of
the Roman Pontiff," it now read: "The Infallible Magisterium of
the Roman Pontiff." The council thus acknowledged as correct
Guidi's point that infallibility is not a habitual property of the
person of the pope; it is rather, connected with specific magisterial acts. Furthermore, the deputation inserted into the chapter
the section on human means, thus taking account of Ketteler's
suggestion.[33]

On July 9, 1870, the revised text was presented to the fathers
of the council. It satisfied neither the minority nor the majority;
indeed, it seems to have aggravated the polarization. The moderate bishops on both sides regarded it as acceptable in principle,

---

31. M 52, 1041 BD.
32. M 52, 1188–93.
33. See Schatz, *Vaticanum I*, 3:133–38.

because it no longer taught a personal, separate, and absolute infallibility.[34] This judgment, insofar as it was shared by bishops of the minority, is important for the interpretation of Vatican I. Of the minority group, a majority of them decided, for tactical reasons, to reject the text — although some members of the minority suggested giving conditional agreement to the new text, thus leaving room for last-minute improvements.

A provisional vote on July 13, 1870, had the following result: Of the 601 council fathers, 401 voted for the text and 88 against it, while 62 agreed *iuxta modum,* requesting a modification. Of the 62 conditional approvals, the requests of 32 placed them among the minority. Six of these requests had to do with the section on the use of human means; they demanded that their use be mentioned, not as a fact of the past, as in the text, but as a norm for the future.[35]

The minority initially celebrated the large number of rejections as a success for their cause. However, their reaction proved to be a great mistake, because the rejections caused many bishops of the majority and, above all, Pius IX to harden their positions. Given this situation, some of the council fathers succeeded in inducing the pope to intervene directly. On his instruction, and without further debate in a plenary assembly, the *Deputation on the Faith* added to the existing words of the definition: "...that such definitions of the Roman Pontiff are therefore irreformable of themselves" these further words: "...and not because of the consent of the church" (*ex sese, non autem ex consensu Ecclesiae,* ND 839). In principle, this addition changed nothing in the content of the definition, but disillusionment with this surprise maneuver and with the behavior of the pope caused many bishops of the minority to leave the council ahead of schedule. On July 18, 1870, the constitution *Pastor Aeternus* passed with 533 yeas and 6 nays.[36]

---

34. Ibid., 138–40.
35. Ibid., 147–52.
36. Ibid., 152–67.

The Definition of the Pope's Infallible Magisterium

Immediately before the provisional vote, in which the minority were still taking part, Bishop Gasser, the spokesman for the *Deputation on the Faith*, explained the revised text. He endeavored to address the concerns and misgivings of the minority and to win its agreement. This was at a point in time when an agreement still seemed possible. His very detailed remarks, which took three hours, showed where and how the deputation accommodated the minority and where the limits were. For this reason, and as a statement representative of the deputation, his commentary is the most important help we have for interpreting the dogma of infallibility.[37]

The definition of the infallibility of the papal magisterium reads as follows:

> It is a divinely revealed dogma that the Roman Pontiff when he speaks *ex cathedra*, that is, when, acting in the office of shepherd and teacher of all Christians, he defines, by virtue of his supreme apostolic authority, a doctrine concerning faith or morals to be held by the universal Church, possesses through the divine assistance promised to him in the person of Blessed Peter, the infallibility with which the divine Redeemer willed his Church to be endowed in defining the doctrine concerning faith and morals, and that such definitions of the Roman Pontiff are therefore irreformable of themselves, not because of the consent of the Church [*ex sese, non autem ex consensu ecclesiae*). (ND 839]

Was the infallibility here being defined the absolute, separate, and personal infallibility against which the minority had taken up arms from the outset? The answer must be no, as indeed even the moderate members of the minority finally realized. But it is not an unqualified no.

The council did not define an *absolute* infallibility of the pope, as the extreme infallibilists wanted. The latter rejected every limitation on the pope and his infallibility. Against them the spokesman for the deputation explained:

---

37. M 52, 1204–30.

> Absolute infallibility belongs only to God, the first and essential
> truth who can never deceive or be deceived in any way. All other
> infallibility, by the fact that it is communicated for a certain end,
> has limits and conditions by which it is judged to be present. This is
> true also of the infallibility of the Roman Pontiff.[38]

Thus understood, the definition limits the infallibility of the
papal magisterium in three ways: In its active subject, its object,
and its act.

Infallibility is limited in regard to its *active subject:* only when
the pope speaks *ex cathedra,* that is, when he acts in the office of
shepherd and teacher of all Christians. Gasser here explains that
the pope is given the gift of inerrancy only in his relationship to
the entire church. Outside of that relationship, and as a private
teacher, he does not possess the charism of truth.

The pope's infallibility is also limited in regard to its *object:*
only when he defines a doctrine concerning faith or morals. Thus
he can only define what is part of apostolic tradition and the
common faith of the church. In the corresponding chapter the
text reads:

> For the Holy Spirit was not promised to the successors of Peter that
> they might disclose a new doctrine by his revelation, but rather, that,
> with his assistance, they might jealously guard and faithfully explain
> the revelation or deposit of faith that was handed down through the
> apostles. (ND 836)

As the spokesman explained, the possible object of infallible
decisions also includes those truths which are necessarily required
in order that the deposit of revelation may be truly preserved,
rightly expounded, and effectively determined, even though these
truths are not revealed as such.[39] According to the information
provided by Gasser, the precise determination of this so-called
"secondary object" of infallibility was to be made only in the
Second Constitution on the Church, because the scope of the infallibility of the church and that of the pope is the same.[40] For, as
is said in the definition, the pope possesses "the infallibility with

---

38. M 52, 1214 A.
39. M 52, 1226 B.
40. M 52, 1226f.; 1316 CD.

which the divine Redeemer willed his church to be endowed in defining the doctrine concerning faith and morals." However, the Second Constitution on the Church was not to be passed, so the question of the "secondary object" of infallibility remained open at the end of the council. In order, however, to leave the question open and not to limit infallibility to revealed truths, the text of the definitions uses the words "to be held" instead of "to be believed."

Finally, infallibility is limited in regard to the *act:* only when the pope defines, by virtue of his supreme apostolic authority, a doctrine to be held by the universal church. As Gasser's important commentary makes clear, an *ex cathedra* decision must be distinct, not only from private utterances of the pope, but also from teaching which the pope presents as supreme leader of the church but to which he does not intend to bind the faithful in a definitive way. In *ex cathedra* decisions the pope must expressly declare his intention of passing a definitive judgment and obliging the entire church to hold to the teaching in question.[41] This limitation represented progress, since it had not been contained in the drafts.

Another advance was represented by the fact that the formulation of the definition repeatedly seeks to make it clear that it is not the person of the pope, but his acts, that are infallible and his decisions that are irreformable. Thus we read in the definition: "when he speaks," "acting in the office of shepherd and teacher," "in defining," "such definitions . . . are therefore irreformable." Gasser explains here that the pope has the privilege of inerrancy, not simply by reason of his office, but only insofar as he has the special help of God in specific actions. Of course, he always possesses his office as supreme judge in matters of faith and morals, but his inerrancy is limited to precisely specified actions.[42] As the outlines for his address that are contained in his papers make clear, Gasser was desirous at this point of making his own the main argument in Guidi's address.[43]

---

41. M 52, 1225 C.
42. M 52, 1213 AB.
43. See Horst, *Unfehlbarkeit und Geschichte*, 205 n. 112.

In two ways, therefore, the infallibility here defined is not a "personal" infallibility. It is given to the pope neither as a private person nor as his habitual property. It can be called "personal" only in the sense that it is promised to the pope by virtue of his office, for specific acts, and not to the Roman church or the Apostolic See, as the Gallicans claimed.[44]

A more difficult question is whether or not Vatican I defined a "separate" infallibility. The text itself says that such definitions of the Roman Pontiff are irreformable, of themselves, and not from the consent of the church. Since the issue for the minority was the organic union of pope, bishops, and church, their main concern was focused on this point. For this reason, the spokesman for the deputation devoted the longest part of his commentary to it.

He insisted that there was question here, not of a separation, but of a distinction. The pope is the center of ecclesiastical unity, and it is his task to preserve this unity and, if it is disrupted, to restore it. His task, therefore, presupposes a special and distinct privilege that has its justification in the special promise of Christ to Peter. Only in this sense is it possible to speak of a separate infallibility. But the special privilege does not separate the pope from the church, because he has his infallibility only as supreme teacher and representative of the church and never defines a doctrine except as this ultimate authority.

Nor do we release the pope, Gasser continued, from the need for cooperation and collaboration with the church, at least not in the sense that such cooperation is excluded.[45] The pope will normally become active only when disputes over the faith cannot be settled at the regional level and when, for this reason, the bishops are compelled to seek help from the pope as a last resort. Gasser thus emphasized the subsidiary character of the pope's dogmatic decrees, as the minority had wished.

Because the infallibility of the pope is not based on inspiration, there is, even in principle, according to Gasser, a need for the advice and collaboration of the church. Among the appropri-

---

44. M 52, 1212 C.
45. M 52, 1213 C.

ate means of ascertaining the truth the councils take first place, but use is also to be made of the advice of cardinals, bishops, and theologians. However, this necessity is not to be understood as a condition for validity, nor may the manner of consultation be fixed, since it depends on the circumstances of each occasion. We must, rather, trust that the promised assistance includes the pledge that the necessary means will be used.

When Gasser spoke at this point of the need, in principle, for consultation and cooperation, he was attempting to accommodate the minority. However — and this was the limit of the accommodation — this necessity was not to be mentioned in the definition itself. At work here was the traumatic experience of Gallicanism. In any case, when Gasser spoke of a need in principle, he was going further than the corresponding section in the chapter, which speaks of the means of determining truth only with reference to the past:

> For their part, the Roman Pontiffs, according as the conditions of the times and the circumstances dictated, sometimes by calling together ecumenical Councils or sounding out the mind of the Church throughout the world, sometimes through regional Councils, or sometimes by using other helps which divine Providence supplied, have defined as having to be held those matters which, with the help of God, they had found consonant with the Holy Scripture and with the apostolic Tradition. (ND 835)

Nor, said Gasser finally, do we separate the pope from the consent of the church, whether prior or subsequent consent. For this consent can never be lacking, since it is impossible that the head should be separated from its body.

The minority, however, had insisted that the pope must establish the consent of the church primarily through the active cooperation of the bishops, because the latter are official witnesses and teachers and have a collegial co-responsibility for the entire church. This point, too, Gasser took up.

The necessity of an agreement and active cooperation on the part of the bishops cannot be taken as a condition set by the divine constitution of the church. Luke 22:32 shows, rather, that Peter is to strengthen the brothers and not the other way around.

When some persons speak of reciprocal ties between head and members, this is simply a figurative manner of speaking and not an argument. The relationship of bishops to pope is, rather, that of disciples to teacher.[46]

This one-sided emphasis on the relationship of the pope to bishops could be interpreted in light of extreme infallibilist theory, according to which the infallibility of the pope resides solely in the pope, who communicates it to the church. Gasser explicitly distanced himself from this theory. Jurisdiction, he said, can indeed be shared, but not infallibility. Christ has, in fact, given infallibility both to the entire magisterium of the church, that is, to the apostles together with Peter, and also to Peter in a special promise.[47]

Although Gasser was here emphasizing the participation of the bishops in the office of teaching the universal church, this did not affect his line of argument. This became clear again when he took up a further argument of the minority. The minority had objected that the consent of the church on the faith and on teaching is a rule of faith that binds even the pope. Gasser agreed with this, but again rejected the conclusion drawn by the minority, namely, that the pope must ascertain this consensus with the help of the bishops before issuing a definition. For, said Gasser, the pope can determine the consensus in the church in other ways, for example, with the help of the theologians or by his own efforts. In any case, there could, in Gasser's view, be no question of a strict and absolute necessity to consult the bishops.[48] In particular cases, a council or other form of episcopal collaboration may be very advisable or even necessary. In such cases, Gasser said, this collaboration could very well be opportune and relatively necessary. Gasser's reasons cannot be entirely rejected. The bishops of the minority who insisted on the strict and absolute necessity to consult had not been well advised. Their demand could in fact be understood as a division of sovereignty, as in Maret's proposals, or as a juridical condition for the validity of papal decisions, as in

---

46. M 52, 1216 AB.
47. M 52, 1216 BC.
48. M 52, 1216 D–1217 A.

Gallicanism. But what most members of the minority had in mind was not the absolute necessity of episcopal collaboration in all circumstances, but the admission, in principle, of their collegial co-responsibility as official witnesses and teachers of the church. The issue for them, then, was the theologically founded, essential appropriateness and necessity, in principle, of their collaboration. Gasser affirmed both of these: the participation of the bishops in the infallible teaching office and the necessity, in principle, of their collaboration.

However, the majority had also been poorly advised. Their refusal to express this necessity in principle and this essential appropriateness of consultation in the definition itself was by no means necessary. It would have been enough explicitly to exclude a possible misunderstanding of such an expression on Gallican lines and to link with them Ketteler's proposal in the second of his four principles. Because the majority closed its mind to this possibility of agreement with the minority, they thwarted the agreement that had almost been reached. By acting as they did, they also contributed to the maximalist interpretation of the infallibility dogma, which largely prevailed after the council.

Another answer of Gasser's shows the extent to which the majority were captives of the anti-Gallican and one-sidedly juridical outlook. When he denied the reciprocal character of the relationship between pope and bishops, the statement was indeed correct at the level of jurisdiction and thus applied also to the jurisdictional aspect of the teaching office. However, Gasser did not take account of the complex nature of a magisterial decree, as this had been explained by Guidi. For at the level of witness there is indeed a reciprocal relationship between pope and bishops. In this area the bishops are not the disciples of the pope, but both pope and bishops are witnesses who give testimony to one another about the faith of their churches and of the church as a whole. This vision of the relation between pope and bishops as one of a teacher to students was one of the causes of the doctrinal centralization that arose.

Another passage also shows clearly that Gasser's answer to the concern of the minority was oversimplified. The minority had said that it must be made clear to everyone whether and how the pope bases himself on the common faith of the church. To this end, the obligation of the pope to a diligent and careful consultation had to be expressly mentioned. Gasser insisted that the diligence and care with which the pope had to investigate the common faith of the church was a moral obligation binding the conscience of the pope, but did not represent a juridical condition. In addition, according to Gasser, the charism of truth does not depend on the private conscience of the pope (which God alone knows) but on his public relationship (*publica relatio*) to the church as a whole. Otherwise, the gift of infallibility would not be an effective means of preserving or restoring the unity of the church. Gasser was correct in saying that when the church trusts in the efficacy of the commission and promise given to Peter, it is relying ultimately on the power and fidelity of God and not on the conscience of the pope. However, if the relationship of the pope to the church as a whole is a public one, as Gasser explained, then it too is subject to the conditions affecting a public relationship, which must be visible.

One of these conditions is that it must be publicly visible and ascertainable whether and how the pope is connected with the common faith of the church. Therefore the inner certainty of the pope's conscience is not enough. If this certainty is not made clear to the public, the pope's decision may not lack truth but it will lack credibility. For this reason the minority insisted on the public discovery of the measures the pope takes in ascertaining the truth. The minority thought that the most appropriate means to this end was consultation with, or the agreement of, the episcopate. Since good theological and pastoral reasons for this request exist, it becomes clear once again that strategic motives played the decisive role in the rejection and were the real hindrance to a meeting of minds. It would not be until Vatican II that this concern of the minority would be accepted.

It remains to examine the formula "of themselves, not from the consent of the Church" (*ex sese, non autem ex consensu Ecclesiae*) in the light of Gasser's commentary. At the time when Gasser was explaining the text of the definition, the text included

only the words "of themselves." When this formula was, at the
last moment, expanded to included "not from the consent of the
Church," Gasser remarked only that the addition simply put neg-
atively what the words "of themselves" already expressed in a
positive way.[49] In the period that followed, however, the formula
acquired great importance, because it became for the maximalists the password for their interpretation of the dogma and, for
others, the peg on which to hang their criticism of the dogma.
How, then, is the formula to be understood in the context of
the definition and in the light of the explanations given by the
spokesman for the Deputation on the Faith?

The negative formula, "not from the consent of the Church,"
was intended to exclude the teaching that the formal consent
of the episcopate or the church is absolutely necessary if an *ex
cathedra* decision of the pope is to be irreformable.

The formula is not meant to say that the cooperation or consultation of the episcopate and the church in the preparation of
an *ex cathedra* decision is not necessary in principle, or not in
every case, or that it is not highly appropriate. Nor is it meant to
say that the consent of the church in the past and the present is
not a binding rule of faith even for the pope.

The formula cannot exclude the principle that a formal refusal
of consent by the entire church, including the episcopate, would
be a sign that there has been no *ex cathedra* decision.[50]

The intent of the positive formula "of themselves" is to say
that the irreformability of an *ex cathedra* decision is based on the
special commission and promise given by Christ to Peter and on
the corresponding divine assistance, which, for the sake of the
entire church, preserves the pope from error in issuing such a
definition.

Even in light of Gasser's explanations, the addition of the
words "not from the consent of the Church" to the phrase "of

---

49. M 52, 1317 AB.

50. See Joseph Ratzinger, *Das neue Volk Gottes* (Düsseldorf: Patmos, 1969), 144;
Walter Kasper, "Zur Diskussion um das Problem der Unfehlbarkeit," in Hans Küng,
ed., *Fehlbar? Eine Zwischenbilanz* (Zürich: Benziger, 1973), 84; Avery Dulles,
A Church to Believe In: Discipleship and the Dynamic of Freedom (New York:
Crossroad, 1987), 139.

themselves" must be judged to be theologically misleading. The reason is that it presents as mutually exclusive two statements that are on entirely different levels. "Of themselves" refers to the divine promise and assistance, while "not from the consent of the Church" refers to the cooperation and consent of the church. Arguing that infallibility is not based on inspiration, Gasser had explained that divine assistance and the cooperation of the church are not in conflict; on the contrary, they are interconnected. Guidi too had explained, along the same line, that consultation and cooperation are inherent phases in the making of a definition. Furthermore, Gasser had explained that papal definitions cannot lack the consent of the church; there is here, then, no opposition involving an exclusion. The contrast has meaning only in the juridical sphere as signifying two mutually exclusive legal titles or grounds of validity; in other words, it has meaning only as a condemnation of Gallican teaching. But this condemnation would have been more effective in the form of a separate canon clearly naming the error than in this theologically misleading insertion.

In conclusion, it may be said that Gasser's explanations merit a detailed study. As a statement of the Deputation on the Faith they are the most important aid we have for a correct interpretation of the infallibility dogma. Moreover, in his observations Gasser represents the viewpoint of the more outstanding members of the majority that ultimately won out. These bishops dissociated themselves from the extreme views of the infallibilists and were ready for some agreement with the minority. However, they remained locked into anti-Gallicanism and the antiliberal principle of authority. Conditioned by this outlook, they only partially understood the theological concerns of the minority, or else for strategic reasons refused to admit the suggestions of the minority into the definition itself.

Gasser's observations also show that it was not always easy for him to find good reasons for turning down many proposals of the minority. His observations also show that the following points were not rejected simply because of the silence concerning them in the definition: the duty of the pope to consult; the appropriateness and necessity, in principle, of collaboration with the bishops; and the subsidiary character of a papal definition.

Finally, Gasser's explanations are very important because Vatican II repeatedly referred back to them and even took a number of his formulations into the text of its constitution on the church for the purpose of excluding a maximalist interpretation of the dogma of infallibility.

At Vatican I the contribution of the minority was to prevent the extreme infallibilist conception of an absolute or *a priori* papal infallibility from prevailing. As a result, despite its one-sided formulations, the dogma of the infallibility of the papal magisterium remained open to being reformulated in the context of an ecclesiology of communion.

Three Interpretations of the Infallibility Dogma

Little attention has been paid to the fact that in the period between the First and the Second Vatican Councils three different interpretations of infallibility coexisted more or less peacefully.[51] This fact can be seen especially in the pastoral letters and publications of the council fathers after Vatican I.[52]

Given the preceding analysis, the coexistence of different interpretations is easily explained. The constitution *Pastor Aeternus* excluded any denial of papal infallibility, but did not exclude the three conceptions of it that were at odds with each other at the council. As a result, the three conceptions which existed at the council could persist afterwards as three different interpretations of the dogma.

The first, the maximalist interpretation, corresponded to the conception held by the extreme infallibilist group at the council. Its core was the doctrine that the infallible authority of the pope is the source of the infallibility of the church. In this view, the

---

51. See Hermann J. Pottmeyer, "Das Unfehlbarkeitsdogma im Streit der Interpretationen," in Karl Lehmann, ed., *Das Petrusamt* (Munich: Schnell & Steiner, 1982), 89–109.

52. See Schatz, *Vaticanum I*, 3:283–96.

pope is the real teacher of the church; all others, including the bishops, are primarily hearers and heeders. There is no need of consultation with, or the collaboration of, the episcopate in the development of church teaching or in the definition of a dogma.

The danger in this interpretation is that it makes papal infallibility almost a matter of inspiration. It pays little heed to the collegial structure of the ecclesiastical magisterium. It tends to blur the lines between an infallible *ex cathedra* decision and the other doctrinal utterances of the pope. In consequence, this leads to what is called "sweeping infallibility" or "galloping infallibility." It calls for one-way communication in the church and for doctrinal centralization.

As a theological theory and in a pure form, the maximalist interpretation was indeed held by only a few. However, as a tendency, and especially in practice, it has been successful. In the public mind, and among many Catholics, it frequently determined, and still determines, the understanding of Vatican I's dogma of infallibility. The maximalist interpretation is incompatible with an ecclesiology of communion.

The second, or middle-ground, interpretation corresponds to the line followed by the majority at Vatican I and is also to be seen in Gasser's explanations. It keeps strictly to the wording of the council, distinguishes itself from the maximalist interpretation, and rejects the widespread misunderstandings of papal infallibility. Until Vatican II this middle-ground view was the most widespread interpretation of the dogma.

This middle-ground interpretation is unsatisfactory in that it shares the one-sided emphasis in the statement of the dogma itself. By limiting itself to the wording of the definition, it does not bring out the fact that the council did not intend the definition to be taken as a comprehensive theology of the ecclesiastical magisterium; with an eye to the situation of that day, it aimed primarily at condemning Gallicanism and strengthening papal authority. As a result, this interpretation fosters the likelihood that what the council did not want to go into for strategic reasons or to include in the definition will seem either nonexistent or theologically unimportant. Included in what is thus passed over is, above all, the doctrine of the collegial structure of the church's teaching office, the doctrine of the "sense of faith" which all the faithful have, and the importance of the credibility of the church's doctrinal utterances and their reception into the life of the church. Whereas the council fathers of Vatican I were still fully aware of the traditional teaching on the collegiality of the teaching office and the importance of the consensus of the church and took this for granted, all this is now falling into oblivion.

The danger of the middle-ground interpretation of the infallibility dogma was and is that it encourages the same tendency and practice as does the maximalist interpretation. The two interpretations have in common that they are concerned to ensure an effective exercise of papal authority. In practice, the middle-ground interpretation has promoted a doctrinal centralization far more effectively than has the maximalist interpretation because it does not reveal that the one-sidedness of the infallibility dogma was motivated chiefly by strategic considerations. However, it is distinguished from the maximalist interpretation by the fact that it, like the definition itself, remains open to a reformulation of papal infallibility in the context of an ecclesiology of communion.

Finally, the third interpretation corresponds to the concerns of the minority at the council. The minority's understanding of the infallibility dogma requires our special attention for two reasons: first, because for a long time it received little attention; second, because it is undoubtedly indebted to a communion ecclesiology. This interpretation reflects more strongly the tradition of the first millennium like the Vatican I minority itself. According to this interpretation, the church is first and foremost a community of churches that are led by the bishops in communion with the pope. The pope is first and foremost the head of the college of bishops, and the church of Rome is the center of church unity. Together with the pope the bishops are responsible, not only for their particular churches, but for the unity of the whole church.

The interpretation of infallibility is located in the setting of this overall conception of the church. Infallibility in faith and teaching is promised primarily to the church as a whole. Infallibility is, therefore, given to the pope and the college of bishops only for the sake of the entire church and in relation to the entire church. They teach infallibly only when they inform themselves regarding apostolic tradition, which is attested in the scriptures and the tradition of the church. In order that the authority of the church's teaching office may be credible, the entire church must be able to ascertain whether, and how, the pope and bishops are relying on scripture, tradition, and the consensus of the church. The primary place for issuing a magisterial decision is a council, which is infallible being representative of the church, its faith, and its teaching office.

An *ex cathedra* decision of the pope, which is likewise infallible, is appropriate only when there is no other way of preserving or restoring the unity of the church in faith and doctrine; it is, by its nature, subsidiary. If the pope acts in this way, he acts as visible head and mouth of the church and as head of the episcopal college by reason of his commission as successor of Peter. This relationship finds expression in the fact that in preparing an *ex cathedra* decision he makes sure of the cooperation of the bishops, who are likewise official witnesses and teachers of the common faith.

The interpretation given by the minority bishops had another point in common with the tradition of the first millennium: the priority which they assigned to witness, over jurisdiction, in the area of teaching. In a magisterial act, witness and jurisdiction are inseparably connected. However, witness, which attests to the true faith, takes priority over jurisdiction since an act of the magisterium aims primarily at truth and, only then, at obedience which is owed to the truth alone. The greater the number of witnesses behind a testimony and the more extensive the consent, the more a testimony will guarantee the truth. These principles, which lay behind the principle of consensus that was followed in the church of the first millennium, do not lose their validity due to the infallibility dogma. The pope, as visible head of the church, acts independently in the exercise of his primacy of jurisdiction; however, in an *ex cathedra* decision, insofar as this must be a testimony to the common faith, he is not independent of the church as a community of witnesses. Given this conception of things, an absolute infallibility or a doctrinal sovereignty of the pope is unthinkable, and that reason was the most important motive of the resistance of the minority.

As the debate at the council showed, many members of the minority confused the necessity, in principle, of episcopal cooperation with its absolute necessity in every case and in all circumstances. As a result, they were in danger of basing the infallibility of an *ex cathedra* decision, not on the divine assistance, but on the cooperation and consent of the bishops. The debate served to make clear that divine assistance and cooperation or consultation are not in competition with each other and that, on the contrary, God's assistance includes an appropriate participation of the bishops; recognition of this fact is incompatible with a doctrinal centralization.

In the final days of the council leading members of the minority were of the opinion that the definition in its final form no longer assumed a separate and absolute infallibility of the pope. For this reason they thought it possible to accept it. Since they saw their understanding of the matter as no longer excluded by the definition, they gave their approval either at the final vote or after the council. However, they were not happy about the definition because it did not express their concern.

When the bishops saw their interpretation as not excluded, they had in mind the section which spoke of the practice of the popes in past ages of availing themselves of the cooperation of the bishops and the church. The only question was whether this description of earlier practice was also normative for the future. Many of the maximalists denied that it was, claiming that councils and other forms of cooperation had now been rendered superfluous. At this point, the minority bishops were aided by a book of Bishop Joseph Fessler. His voice carried special weight because he had belonged to the majority and, in addition, had been secretary of the council. He explained that the section in question was essential for the interpretation of the dogma of infallibility, because in the future, too, the popes would act in the way described.[53] His statement established, at least in an indirect way, the normative significance of the section.

Crucial, however, was the fact that Fessler received a letter from Pius IX in which the latter stated that in his book Fessler had correctly conveyed the true meaning of the dogma of papal infallibility.[54] It was on the basis of this letter that some of the hesitating minority bishops finally subscribed to the dogma.

A further indirect confirmation of this interpretation was Pius IX's praise of the Collective Declaration of the German bishops, in 1875, as an accurate representation of the conciliar decrees.[55]

As all of this shows, most of the minority bishops were convinced that their understanding of things was compatible with the dogma of infallibility. They agreed to the dogma only as understood in their interpretation of it. This interpretation was tolerated, and even indirectly confirmed, by the papacy.

Only in connection with Vatican II and the preparation for it was more attention paid once again to this interpretation. In fact, it formed an important bridge to Vatican II, which once again took up the concerns of the minority and agreed with them. In this third interpretation, the infallibility dogma of Vatican I is compatible with a communion ecclesiology.

---

53. Joseph Fessler, *The True and False Infallibility of the Popes* (New York: Catholic Publication Society, 1875), 21.

54. See Schatz, *Vaticanum I*, 3:297.

55. See DS 3116.

CHAPTER SIX

Papacy in Communion: Perspectives from Vatican II

Rebellion against Centralization and Emergence from a Ghetto

The Second Vatican Council has left us a building site. It resembles the building site of St. Peter's in the sixteenth century: Alongside the ancient Roman basilica there towered into the heavens the four monumental supporting columns that were later to carry the most beautiful dome in the world, the one that today arches over the tomb of Peter the Apostle.

Like Vatican I, Vatican II was unable to complete its work. While Vatican I was hindered by a war, Vatican II was unable to complete the reform of the church and ecclesiology because the maximalist interpretation of Vatican I, combined with pragmatic concerns, stood in the way. The work of Vatican II has remained a building site. Alongside the old edifice of nineteenth- and twentieth-century Vatican centralization arise the four mighty supporting columns of a renewed church and a renewed ecclesiology: the church as people of God; the church as sacrament of the kingdom of God in the world; the college of bishops; and ecumenism. While the building erected by centralization awaits demolition, as the old St. Peter's Basilica did in its day, the four supporting pillars of a renewed church and a renewed ecclesiology wait to be crowned by the dome that draws them into unity.

The maximalist interpretation of Vatican I supported Vatican centralization and, for a long time, stamped the general consciousness within the church. This interpretation was persuaded that the dogmas of jurisdictional primacy and papal infallibility were the definitive culmination of ecclesiology and the ecclesiastical order. However, on the eve of Vatican II the study of the church fathers and of early church history was already paving the way for a change. The majority of the council fathers at Vatican II had two concerns: to rebel against centralization, and to bring the church out of its ghetto into the modern world.

The first of these concerns, rebellion against centralization, provided the motivation to add to the dogmas of Vatican I a comprehensive doctrine of the church and of the college of bishops. The result was *Lumen gentium,* the Dogmatic Constitution on the Church. Leading the church into the modern world proved to be the more difficult task. This effort yielded *Gaudium et spes,* the Pastoral Constitution on the Church in the Modern World. The basic idea followed in *Lumen gentium* is the church as the people of God on pilgrimage; the basic idea in *Gaudium et spes* is the church as the universal sacrament of salvation. The real novelty produced by the council was the pastoral constitution *Gaudium et spes* along with the Decree on Ecumenism and the Declaration on Religious Freedom. The constitution *Lumen gentium,* on the other hand, offers little that is new; yet it takes an important step forward, for it reflects upon the original theology and order of the church in the first millennium. This backward gaze is both its strength and its weakness. It is its strength, because it broke the spell cast by a one-sidedly clerical and juridical vision of the church with its opposition to the Reformation and Gallicanism. This backward gaze is, at the same time, the weakness of *Lumen gentium,* because as a result of looking back, the council's second concern, the emergence into the modern world, receives too little attention in this document.[1]

---

1. See Hermann J. Pottmeyer, "Dogmatic Constitution on the Church," in Richard P. McBrien, ed., *Encyclopedia of Catholicism* (San Francisco: HarperCollins, 1995), 425–27.

The Nightmare of Shared Governance

Proof that the constitution *Lumen gentium* contains little that is new can be found especially in its third chapter, on the hierarchical church. This chapter also deals with the office of the pope. It is in chapter 3 that the continuity with Vatican I is most conspicuous. The discussion of the papal office makes use, almost exclusively, of citations from Vatican I; the doctrine on the college of bishops likewise appeared at Vatican I, although the council did not have the time to define it. The fact that this doctrine is celebrated as a great accomplishment of Vatican II shows how effectively the maximalist interpretation of Vatican I had suppressed this teaching. It is reported that when a great controversy over the doctrine of collegiality arose, Paul VI had to persuade himself by means of study night after night that the doctrine is not opposed to tradition and Vatican I.[2]

The majority at Vatican II was not successful in its attempt to end Vatican centralization by means of its teaching on collegiality. The history of Vatican I is important because it shows how and why the doctrine on collegiality can very well coexist with a concept of the papacy that promotes centralization. At that earlier council the majority had prevented the introduction of the normal appropriateness of cooperation between pope and bishops in important decisions affecting the universal church. The only concern of those bishops was the independence and freedom of action of the pope. From this silence of Vatican I the maximalist interpretation drew the conclusion that centralization was the norm.

Now, at Vatican II, the minority was motivated by the same concern. They objected to saying that the bishops already share in the supreme and universal power of jurisdiction of the episcopal college only by reason of their episcopal consecration. For then, they objected, the bishops would have their power of jurisdiction directly from Christ, and the pope would be obliged to

---

2. See Peter Hebblethwaite, *Paul VI: The First Modern Pope* (New York: Paulist, 1993), 384–92.

let them take part in the government of the universal church. However, they said, such a shared governance contradicts Vatican I, which condemned the teaching of Bishop Maret, namely, that the pope "possesses merely the principal part, and not all the fullness of this supreme power." Moreover, to avoid this error and its consequences, it is not enough to say that the college of bishops possesses supreme jurisdiction only habitually, while its exercise always depends on the pope. For a jurisdiction that cannot be exercised is useless and empty. The minority, therefore, demanded that, as at Vatican I, the question be left open whether the bishops have their collegial jurisdiction directly from Christ or from Christ through the pope.[3] The doctrine that the bishops obtain their entire jurisdiction from the pope had been described by Maret as the key principle of the "absolutist school."

At Vatican II, the criticism of the minority was directed at this sentence: "One is constituted a member of the episcopal body in virtue of the sacramental consecration and by the communion with the head and members of the college" (LG 22). The spokesman for the Doctrinal Commission explained that fear of a shared governance was unfounded, because the next sentence reads: "The college or body of bishops has, for all that, no authority unless united with the Roman Pontiff, Peter's successor, as its head, whose primatial authority, let it be added, over all, whether pastors or faithful, remains in its integrity." However, in order to accommodate the minority, the word "communion" in the objectionable sentence was changed to "hierarchical communion" — an unfortunate addition, since it weakens the idea of communion without actually saying anything new. In addition, it is pointedly said that "together with its head, the Supreme Pontiff, and never apart from him, [the order of bishops] has supreme and full authority over the universal church; but this power cannot be exercised without the agreement of the Roman Pontiff" (LG 22).

---

3. Francisco Gil Hellín, *Concilii Vaticani II Synopsis*, vol. 2: *Constitutio Dogmatica "Lumen Gentium"* (Vatican City: Libreria Editrice Vaticana, 1995), 2061–66.

In order to allay the misgivings of the minority at Vatican II, a further sentence expressly emphasizes the pope's freedom of action: "For the Roman Pontiff, by reason of his office as Vicar of Christ, namely, and as pastor of the entire Church, has full, supreme and universal power over the whole Church, a power which he can always exercise unhindered."

Since the minority at Vatican II still saw a contradiction with Vatican I, Paul VI found himself obliged to intervene directly in order to win the agreement of the minority, which included many members of the Roman Curia. After the council, the pope said, there should be no victors and vanquished.

By the famous "Preliminary Explanatory Note"[4] the Doctrinal Commission had to notify the following clarification of chapter 3 to the council fathers: "The word *College* . . . does not imply *equality* between the head and members of the college, but only a proportion between the two relationships: Peter – apostles and pope – bishops." The special place of the pope in the college of bishops was underscored by this clarification and by the expression "hierarchical communion." Two further remarks brought out the pope's freedom of action: "The Roman Pontiff undertakes the regulation, encouragement, and approval of the exercise of collegiality as he sees fit for the well-being of the church"; and: "The Pope, as supreme pastor of the church, may exercise his power at any time, as he sees fit, by reason of the demands of his office." The spokesman for the Doctrinal Commission explained that the "Preliminary Note" was not an integral part of the constitution but "that it is according to the mind and sense of this note that the teaching contained in chapter 3 is to be explained and understood."

In the constitution and the note, the minority succeeded in having the pope's independence and freedom of action stressed in a way that these had not been emphasized even in the Vatican I definition. Analysis of Vatican I has shown that this earlier council had avoided every reference to a collegial collaboration

---

4. "Preliminary Explanatory Note" in Austin Flannery, ed., *Vatican Council II: The Conciliar and Post Conciliar Documents* (Dublin: Dominican Publications, 1988), 424–26.

of the episcopate in the governing of the universal church; it had done so for strategic reasons, namely, out of fear that such references could be misunderstood along Gallican lines. This fear had become groundless by the time of Vatican II. Why, then, was this action taken now, and for what reasons?

The reasons can be gathered from the already cited arguments of the Vatican II minority. The first reason was the maximalist interpretation of Vatican I and especially of the statement in the canon directed against Maret. The second reason was the fear that the pope would no longer be free to govern the church if the bishops had a right to share in the government. Since the leading members of the minority of Vatican II were also members of the Roman Curia, the pragmatic character of this argument is obvious. These men were afraid of losing their own shared governance with the pope.

Regarding "the nightmare of shared governance," council theologian Joseph Ratzinger observed at that time: "the special position of the pope, dogmatically defined in 1870...is in no way challenged" by a synod of bishops, such as was suggested by the council, or by other forms of episcopal participation in the government of the universal church. For there has always been some form of shared governance in practice: "In antiquity it was that of the synods, in the Middle Ages that of the Consistory of Cardinals; in modern times...the sharing in government by the bureaucracy and the curial machine."[5] Ratzinger also criticized the "combining of practical concerns and theological questions" in the debate on collegiality. It was necessary, he said, "to prevent an ideologizing of the pragmatic" and "to let the pragmatic remain pragmatic and to see clearly how narrow the area of divine law is in the church and how broad the scope for discretion is."[6]

After Vatican I centralization and the maximalist interpretation of the primacy of jurisdiction had relied on the silence of that council on the subject of collegial co-responsibility. On the

---

5. Joseph Ratzinger, "Konkrete Formen bischöflicher Kollegialität," in Johann Chr. Hampe, ed., *Ende der Gegenreformation? Das Konzil, Dokumente und Deutung* (Stuttgart: Kreuz, 1964), 160.

6. Ibid., 155f.

contrary, after Vatican II, people thought they could now re-
tain centralization by appealing to the frequent emphasis laid on
papal independence and freedom of action in the texts of this new
council. Thus the fear of a shared governance by bishops, which
according to the Roman Curia had to be prevented at any cost,
determined the texts of Vatican II.

The conception of the primacy of jurisdiction as sovereignty
was also present and active in the texts of Vatican II with their
one-sided emphasis on the pope's freedom of action. This concept could exist alongside the teaching on the college of bishops,
because the exercise of collegial jurisdiction depends entirely on
the pope. At the very least, it is striking that nothing is said with
comparable clarity about the obligation of the pope to involve
the bishops in decisions affecting the universal church. We cannot
help but think of such an obligation, when it comes, for example,
to the passing of laws for the universal church. Is not such legislation a matter also of the collegial co-responsibility of the bishops
for the universal church, and does it not interfere with their ordinary and immediate jurisdiction over the particular churches,
and this to such a degree that it should not occur without the
participation of the bishops? But for the minority at Vatican II
such an obligation would have been an instance precisely of the
shared governance it feared, for they understood such shared
government as a division of the primacy of jurisdiction, as the
maximalist interpretation of Vatican I saw it.

In contrast, the ideas of the majority at Vatican II moved in
the direction of some form of permanent participation of the
bishops in the leadership of the church. The council decreed the
establishment of a synod of bishops. "This council, as it will be
representative of the whole Catholic episcopate, will bear testimony to the participation of all the bishops in hierarchical
communion in the care of the universal church."[7] The rights of
bishops to collaborate fell far short of the original ideas of the
majority when Paul VI, in 1965, formally established the synod

---

7. Decree on the Pastoral Office of Bishops in the Church, *Christus Dominus*,
no. 5; see Patrick Granfield, *The Limits of the Papacy: Authority and Autonomy in
the Church* (New York: Crossroad, 1987), 88–97.

of bishops and published the norms for its operation; many of the council fathers expressed disappointment. Those original ideas, too, had fallen victim to the nightmare of shared governance.

Collegiality from Above and Collegiality from Below

In any case, it was a step forward that Vatican II, "following in the steps of the First Vatican Council" (LG 18), now supplemented the teaching on the primacy with its teaching on the office of bishop and on the college of bishops. It was crucial for the concept of the church that the council revived the ancient doctrine of the sacramental and collegial character of the episcopate. Episcopal consecration communicates the office of sanctifying, teaching, and ruling (LG 21), and its possessor is incorporated into the college of bishops (LG 22). Therefore, the college of bishops likewise has the office of teaching and ruling the universal church in communion with the pope as head — due to the episcopal consecration of its members and, thus, immediately from Christ. The minority correctly saw that this doctrine called into question the fundamental principle in the maximalist conception of the primacy, according to which all episcopal jurisdiction comes immediately from the pope.

The sacramental foundation of the college of bishops and of its divine right reflected the biblical origin of the college. "Just as, in accordance with the Lord's decree, St. Peter and the rest of the apostles constitute a unique apostolic college, so, in like fashion, the Roman Pontiff, Peter's successor, and the bishops, the successors of the apostles, are related with and united to one another" (LG 22). This biblical justification is followed by justification from the tradition of the early church: The church has always showed itself to be a communion of churches that are collegially linked to one another and with the bishop of Rome.

In these texts two ways of constructing the idea of collegiality can be seen, as Joseph Ratzinger correctly noted.[8] One way

---

8. Joseph Ratzinger, "Die bischöfliche Kollegialität: Theologische Entfaltung,"

begins with the universal church, for which the college of bishops, with the pope as its head, is responsible. The bishops are not members of the college insofar as they are the shepherds of particular churches; rather, they are shepherds of particular churches because they are members of the college of bishops. This corresponds to the biblical argument that the episcopal college as a whole succeeded to the apostolic college. The main concern in this approach is to move beyond Vatican centralization by striking a balance between the supreme and full jurisdiction of the pope and the supreme and full jurisdiction of the college of bishops. Ratzinger points to Karl Rahner as a representative of this approach and characterizes it as a doctrine of collegiality that is modern and speculative in tendency.

In contrast, Ratzinger goes on to make his own the understanding of collegiality found in the early church and in the church fathers. This approach takes as its starting point the particular or local church; it understands the universal church to be a community or communion of churches (*communio ecclesiarum*), and this communion to be the source of collegiality. The individual church is not simply a part of the universal church, but is itself truly church because it becomes a church through the hearing of God's word and the celebration of the Eucharist. As such, it is a member of the communion of churches that manifests itself in the communion of the bishops with each other and with the pope, that is, in the college of bishops. Insofar as a bishop heads an individual church as a successor of the apostles, he is also a member of the college consisting of the other successors of the apostles. The pope does not simply happen to be also the bishop of Rome; on the contrary, it is precisely because he is bishop of the church of Rome, which preserves the heritage of Peter and whose bishop is the successor of Peter, that he is a member and head of the college of bishops and visible head of the church.

This communion of pope and bishops is an image of the

---

in Guilherme Baraúna, ed., *De Ecclesia: Beiträge zur Konstitution "Über die Kirche" des 2. Vatikanischen Konzils* (Freiburg: Herder, 1966), 2:55–58; see Thomas Weiler, *Volk Gottes – Leib Christi: Die Ekklesiologie J. Ratzingers und ihr Einfluß auf das 2. Vatikanische Konzil* (Mainz: Grünewald, 1997).

communion of the churches, and the latter, in turn, is an image of the communion of the faithful (*communio fidelium*). The primacy of the pope is a primacy within a communion because he represents and is the concrete embodiment of the universal communion of churches. He needs the catholic witness of the bishops and of the churches and their members, in order to bear witness to, and preserve, the catholicity and unity of the churches.

The main concern of this patristically oriented doctrine of collegiality is to move beyond centralization to a restoration of the communion of churches within the unity of the universal church. Its guiding idea is the biblical and patristic concept of communion, with its threefold meaning: *soteriological* — the communion of the redeemed with God through Jesus Christ in the Holy Spirit; *sacramental-theological* — the communion of the body of Christ, the church, through sharing in word and sacrament, and, in particular, through sharing in the eucharistic body of Christ; and *ecclesiological* — the communion of the churches and the communion of the faithful.

The presence of this patristically orientated approach in the constitution *Lumen gentium* is not as obvious as the presence of the modern one, which catches the eye in the determination of the relationship between primacy and episcopal college. The soteriological meaning (LG 1–4) and the sacramental-theological meaning (LG 3, 7, 9, 11) of communion are to be found primarily in the first and second chapters of the constitution; its meaning as communion of the faithful appears primarily in the second chapter (LG 13).

Special attention is due to the texts that show the ecclesiological meaning of communion as communion of churches. In grounding the collegiality of the episcopate, reference is made directly to the practice of communion in the early church (LG 22). The basis of that practice is the fact that the Catholic Church consists in, and of, the particular churches:

> It is in these [the particular Churches] and formed out of them that the one and unique Catholic Church exists. And for that reason precisely each bishop represents his own Church, whereas all, together

with the pope, represent the whole Church in a bond of peace, love,
and unity. (LG 23)

This fact is, in turn, based on the truth that each particular
church is truly church:

> This Church of Christ is really present in all legitimately organized
> local groups of the faithful, which, in so far as they are united to
> their pastors, are also quite appropriately called Churches in the
> New Testament. For these are in fact, in their own localities, the
> new people called by God, in the power of the Holy Spirit and as
> the result of full conviction (cf. 1 Thess. 1:5). In them the faithful are
> gathered together through the preaching of the Gospel of Christ, and
> the mystery of the Lord's Supper is celebrated, "so that, by means of
> the flesh and blood of the Lord the whole brotherhood of the Body
> may be welded together." In each altar community, under the sa-
> cred ministry of the bishop, a manifest symbol is to be seen of that
> charity and "unity of the mystical body, without which there can
> be no salvation." In these communities, though they may often be
> small and poor, or existing in the diaspora, Christ is present through
> whose power and influence the One, Holy, Catholic and Apostolic
> Church is constituted. For "the sharing in the body and blood of
> Christ has no other effect than to accomplish our transformation
> into that which we receive." (LG 26)

The collegiality of the episcopate therefore takes concrete form
primarily in everyday relations among the particular churches
and among their bishops with one another and with the entire
church:

> Collegiate unity is also apparent in the mutual relations of each
> bishop to individual dioceses and with the universal Church. The
> Roman Pontiff, as successor of Peter, is the perpetual and visi-
> ble source and foundation of the unity both of the bishops and
> of the whole company of the faithful. The individual bishops are
> the visible source and foundation of unity in their own particular
> Churches, which are constituted after the model of the universal
> Church. (LG 23)

It was out of these everyday relations within the community of
churches that corresponding interchurch structures developed at
the regional level, especially the patriarchal churches:

> It has come about through divine providence that, in the course
> of time, different Churches set up in various places by the apostles

and their successors joined together in a multiplicity of organically united groups which, whilst safeguarding the unity of the faith and the unique divine structure of the universal Church, have their own discipline, enjoy their own liturgical usage and inherit a theological and spiritual patrimony. Some of these, notably the ancient patriarchal Churches, as mothers in the faith, gave birth to other daughter-Churches, as it were, and down to our own days they are linked with these by bonds of a more intimate charity in what pertains to the sacramental life and in a mutual respect for rights and obligations. This multiplicity of local Churches, unified in a common effort, shows all the more resplendently the catholicity of the undivided Church. In a like fashion the episcopal conferences at the present time are in a position to contribute in many and fruitful ways to the concrete realization of the collegiate spirit. (LG 23)

From this there emerges within the college of bishops a polar relationship that reflects the interplay of unity and multiplicity in the church:

This college, in so far as it is composed of many members, is the expression of the multifariousness and universality of the People of God; and of the unity of the flock of Christ, in so far as it is assembled under one head. (LG 22)

Clearly visible in these passages are the outlines of an ecclesiology of communion which constitutes here the context of the doctrine on the episcopal college and the primacy. Both forms of the concept of collegiality are important for the development of a primacy in communion; both are present in the texts of the council, and both are concerned with moving beyond centralization.

Ratzinger, too, expressed himself along these lines in 1966. The interplay of the two forms of founding collegiality corresponds, he said, to the reality, which calls for each form, by its nature, to be completed by the other. In answer to criticism from Ratzinger, Rahner said that he, too, saw in the two forms mutually complementary foundations of collegiality. Indeed, Rahner said, the local church is, in fact, being given priority today; however, the development of the modern form is in some degree necessary, and this development can be given a positive interpretation.[9] Years later, in 1983, Ratzinger called Rahner's concept of collegiality "wrong."[10] What was the point of Ratzinger's earlier and later criticism of Rahner?

From the very outset Ratzinger was critical of the modern form, on the grounds that it focused on striking a balance between the supreme jurisdictional power of the pope and that of the bishops; he felt this effort led away from the true idea of collegiality. The controversy over the relationship between these two supreme powers, according to Ratzinger, revolved solely around a borderline case that has little to do with the normal everyday life of the church; collegiality has to be realized primarily within the mutual relationships between the particular churches. Above all, Ratzinger criticizes the focus on the balance between the supreme jurisdiction of the pope and that of the college of bishops because it distracts from the realization that many of the de facto papal functions developed originally from the position of the bishop of Rome as Latin patriarch — functions that have nothing to do with his office as successor of Peter. This realization would open the way along which reform can advance.[11] Here, in fact, Ratzinger offers important pointers for the journey towards a primacy in communion.

Ratzinger's later criticism belongs in the context of reflections on the synod of bishops and of criticism leveled at the deficient juridical organization of the synod. Defending the modest role of the synod of bishops, Ratzinger explains that collegiality does not mean to share the central governance of the universal church. Rather the purpose of the college is to help the church to become a living organism. A bishop does not participate in the direction of the universal church, Ratzinger insists, because he is repre-

9. Karl Rahner, *Schriften zur Theologie*, vol. 8 (Einsiedeln: Benziger, 1967), 425 n. 27; English: "On the Presence of Christ in the Diaspora Community according to the Teaching of the Second Vatican Council," in *Theological Investigations* 10 (New York: Herder and Herder, 1973), 101–2 n. 27.

10. Joseph Ratzinger, "Scopi e metodi del Sinodo dei Vescovi," in Josef Tomko, ed., *Sinodo dei Vescovi: Natura, metodo, prospettive* (Vatican City: Libreria Editrice Vaticana, 1985), 45–58.

11. Joseph Ratzinger, *Ergebnisse und Probleme der dritten Konzilsperiode* (Cologne: Bachem, 1965), 80f.

sented in some central organization. Rather he helps to guide the universal church by the fact that he directs the Catholic Church in the form of his own particular church and that he directs it as a Catholic Church. Those who want to move beyond papal centralization by setting up a collegial central organization alongside the pope would simply introduce a new and worse centralization than that which Vatican II wanted to eliminate.

In this later criticism, Ratzinger draws different conclusions from the basic principles of his ecclesiology of communion than he did earlier. That is, his criticism here contradicts his earlier criticism of the opponents of the synod of bishops, those who conjured up the "nightmare of shared governance." At that time, he pointed out that there had always existed some form of de facto shared governance, especially that of the Roman Curia. Therefore the synod of bishops, being an organ for the collegial collaboration of the episcopate, was meant precisely to replace the shared governance of the Curia, in the original intention of many council fathers. As Ratzinger noted earlier, the Curia as a bureaucratic staff — even doing its best — cannot be an expression of the collegial co-responsibility of the episcopate.

In addition, by limiting the bishops to the leadership of their particular churches, Ratzinger passes over the question: Since legislation for the universal church so extensively shapes the activity of the bishops, does it not call for some participation of the bishops? Does not participation, along the lines of a concept of collegiality based upon the early church, become an obvious need? Is this not true because these laws and the ordinances of the Curia affect, specifically, the everyday life of the particular churches?

Ratzinger had correctly described the concept of collegiality proposed by Rahner as a modern one. As a matter of fact, in this conflict between a form of collegiality based on the early church and the modern form, we meet up again with the distinction between the paradigms of the first and second millennia. As both theologians correctly saw, the two forms need to be brought into a relationship of mutual complementarity; this task of integration, as we have repeatedly seen, is imposed on a broader scale regarding the two paradigms. Although the early church's ecclesiology of communion will likely prove to be more fruitful on the whole for the development of a primacy in communion, Rahner did see a problem which had not yet arisen in the early church.

The early church did not have a central legislation and administration for the universal church. Regulations binding the universal church were made by a council, which was an extraordinary and rare event. The normal administration and regulation of the church's life was done within the patriarchates by the patriarch, together with the bishops or their representatives. However, for the present-day church, which does have a central legislature and administration, Rahner was quite right to ask how to give a collegial character to the central governance of today's universal church. The challenge is not to replace a papal centralization with an episcopal centralization. In dealing with this problem, the separation of the pope's primatial and patriarchal competences is an important element of the solution.

What Vatican II has left us, then, has remained, until today, simply a building site. The council laid the foundations of a renewed ecclesiology and supplied basic elements for the structure of a church that takes the form of a communion of churches. In the practice of the church, too, there have been numerous shifts in the direction of communion and participation. Above all, the council has made us aware of how things ought to be in the church and how we really ought to deal with one another. For the time being, however, what we have is a juxtaposition of different priorities and different ecclesiologies, each with its own emphasis. This is an inevitable source of many conflicts in the church, because legitimate expectations are aroused and then repeatedly disappointed.[12]

As far as the central legislature and administration of the universal church is concerned, we have not yet reached even a shift towards the direction of a shared governance in the spirit of col-

---

12. See Hermann J. Pottmeyer, "A New Phase in the Reception of Vatican II," in Giuseppe Alberigo, Jean-Pierre Jossua, and Joseph A. Komonchak, eds., *The Reception of Vatican II* (Washington, D.C.: Catholic University of America Press, 1987), 27–43.

legiality. The theoretical basis of centralization has indeed been undermined by Vatican II, but its practice continues without interruption.

Papal and Episcopal Infallibility

The last council had little new to add to Vatican I regarding the infallibility of the papal magisterium (LG 25). A step forward was taken, however, when the most important explanations of this dogma by Bishop Gasser were now included in the final text of Vatican II. This represented progress in two respects: for one thing, the maximalist interpretation of this dogma has become almost impossible; for another, the concerns of the minority of Vatican I, committed to an ecclesiology of communion, have been acknowledged.

In order to prevent an absolute and separate infallibility of the pope, the most important concerns of the minority at Vatican I were: In a definition the pope has to be faithful to the scriptures and the faith tradition of the church; he must ascertain this tradition with diligence and by suitable means; and this is to be expressly mentioned as his duty. Vatican II complied with these demands:

> When the Roman Pontiff, or the body of bishops together with him, define a doctrine, they make the definition in conformity with revelation itself, to which all are bound to adhere and to which they are obliged to submit; and this revelation is transmitted integrally either in written form or in oral tradition through the legitimate succession of bishops and above all through the watchful concern of the Roman Pontiff himself; and through the light of the Spirit of truth it is scrupulously preserved in the Church and unerringly explained. The Roman Pontiff and the bishops, by reason of their office and the seriousness of the matter, apply themselves with zeal to the work of enquiring by every suitable means into this revelation and of giving apt expression to its contents; they do not, however, admit any new public revelation as pertaining to the divine deposit of faith. (LG 25)

In addition, Vatican II stated more precisely the meaning of the controversial formula that says the definitions of the pope are

irreformable "of themselves, not from the consent of the Church"
(*ex sese, non autem ex consensu Ecclesiae*):

> His definitions are rightly said to be irreformable by their very na-
> ture and not by reason of the assent of the Church, in as much as
> they were made with the assistance of the Holy Spirit promised to
> him in the person of blessed Peter himself; and as a consequence they
> are in no way in need of the approval of others, and do not admit
> of appeal to any other tribunal. For in such a case the Roman Pon-
> tiff does not utter a pronouncement as a private person, but rather
> does he expound and defend the teaching of the Catholic faith as
> the supreme teacher of the universal Church, in whom the Church's
> charism of infallibility is present in a singular way. (LG 25)

Finally, Vatican II endeavored to integrate the teaching office
of the pope and its infallibility into a context in which the teaching office of the bishops and of the episcopal college was also
discussed. Emphasis was also laid on the point that the infallibility of the teaching office is an expression of that loyalty to the
faith that has been promised to the entire church.

A novelty, in comparison with Vatican I, was that Vatican II
also went into the noninfallible or ordinary magisterium of the
pope, his "authentic teaching authority" (LG 25). In point of
fact, ever since Vatican I this activity of the pope had increased to
an extent hitherto unknown. By means of modern media the pope
as teacher has become present almost everywhere. It was appropriate, therefore, to clarify the binding power of his ordinary
magisterium with its varying degrees. The council calls for "the
loyal submission of the will and intellect," along with "respect,"
to the authentic teaching authority of the pope, and also "that
one sincerely adhere to decisions made by him, conformably
with his manifest mind and intention." Since the council, there
has been widespread discussion of the meaning of these expres-
sions and of the disciplinary measures taken by the Roman Curia
against deviant theological doctrines and teachers; that discussion has not yet ended.[13] Many theologians, and a good many

---

13. See Francis A. Sullivan, *Magisterium: Teaching Authority in the Catholic Church* (New York: Paulist, 1983); Hermann J. Pottmeyer, "Reception and
Submission," in *The Jurist* 51 (1991–93), 269–92; F. A. Sullivan, *Creative Fidelity: Weighing and Interpreting Documents of the Magisterium* (New York:

bishops, are concerned that the development of the church's doctrine is passing entirely into the hands of the pope and the Roman Curia.

It was also natural that, following upon its teaching on the college of bishops, the council should treat of the episcopal college's teaching authority (LG 25). The council distinguishes between the extraordinary exercise of the teaching authority of the episcopal college, in the case of a council, and its ordinary exercise:

> Although the bishops, taken individually, do not enjoy the privilege of infallibility, they do, however, proclaim infallibly the doctrine of Christ on the following conditions: namely, when, even though dispersed throughout the world but preserving for all that amongst themselves and with Peter's successor the bond of communion, in their authoritative teaching concerning matters of faith and morals, they are in agreement that a particular teaching is to be held definitively and absolutely. This is still more clearly the case when, assembled in an ecumenical council, they are, for the universal Church, teachers of and judges in matters of faith and morals, whose decisions must be adhered to with the loyal and obedient assent of faith. (LG 25)

This teaching reflects the doctrine of the full and supreme jurisdiction of the college of bishops and underscores the importance of the collegial magisterium. Its conditions and limitations are the same as those attached to the infallible magisterium of the pope.

However, there is a special difficulty connected with the ordinary and universal magisterium of the whole episcopate: How is it to be established whether the bishops have been unanimous in teaching that a particular doctrine is a divinely revealed truth to which all Catholics are obliged to give a definitive consent of faith? For, in order that a teaching of the ordinary and universal magisterium may be regarded as infallible, this teaching must not only be proposed unanimously, but must also be proposed

Paulist, 1996); Richard R. Gaillardetz, *Teaching with Authority: A Theology of the Magisterium in the Church* (Collegeville, Minn.: Liturgical Press, 1997).

as "to be held definitively and absolutely [*tamquam definitive tenendam*]." It was requested that this condition be specifically included in the text of the council to make a distinction between the infallible and noninfallible teaching.[14] In the past, if there were doubts on this point, the episcopate was consulted or a council was convoked.

Recently, however, another way has been taken. In its statement of November 18, 1995, the Congregation for the Doctrine of the Faith declared that in his apostolic letter *Ordinatio sacerdotalis* of May 30, 1994, the pope had declared the exclusion of women from ordination to the priesthood to be held definitively because this doctrine had been infallibly taught by the ordinary and universal magisterium. In this case, then, the pope had, on his own, and without any explicit consultation of the bishops, ascertained the actual consent of the bishops and its binding nature. He may have had good reasons for acting thus. However, in the ensuing discussion, theologians pointed out that this way of acting could hardly claim to be a convincing embodiment of the collegiality taught by Vatican II.[15]

Because of this and other incidents, there is growing certainty today that Vatican II did not overcome the existing doctrinal centralization. Vatican II had indeed confirmed that the minority at Vatican I was justified in its struggle for an exercise of the teaching office that would bear the stamp of collegiality. However, to a greater extent than was thought in the first enthusiasm after Vatican II, the endeavor of the majority at Vatican I is still operative today; for that majority wanted, above all, to increase the effectiveness of the pope's teaching authority. A good many theologians are of the opinion that, contrary to the intention of the council, the teaching of Vatican II on the ordinary magisterium has even strengthened doctrinal centralization and contributed to new forms of sweeping infallibility. Here again, Vatican II has left us only with a building site.

---

14. Gil Hellín, *Concilii Vaticani II Synopsis,* 256f.
15. See Sullivan, *Creative Fidelity,* 181–84.

Towards a Ministry of Communion
within the Universal Church

We have reached a double conclusion: It is not Vatican I itself but only the maximalist interpretation of its definitions that hinders the development of a papacy in communion; the desire for an ecclesiology of communion was present at Vatican I in the persons of the minority, and this prevented the definition of an absolute and separate papal infallibility.

In the documents of Vatican II the maximalist interpretation (the primacy as sovereignty) is still operative and has prevented a more consistent development of structures that promote communion. Nevertheless, Vatican II does provide the theological foundations for an ecclesiology of communion.

This result explains the persistence of a centralizing structure and practice after Vatican II. The majority of the council fathers intended to overcome centralization; in this regard they failed. The council did not, however, fail in its purpose of bringing the faithful to an awareness that all of us are the church. In many particular churches and regional churches this consciousness has led to structures and a practice of communion and participation.

It is especially in the question of the papacy and its concrete form that Vatican II has left behind what is simply a building site. The Petrine office will acquire its true dimensions only when it becomes a ministry of communion for all churches and Christians. In paving the way to this future for the Petrine office, the following tasks arise on the level of theology.

First, there must be agreement on an ecumenical ecclesiology of communion in all the churches and in the ecumenical dialogue. Only from this perspective will the Petrine office be understood as a ministry of communion — for the community of churches and its unity. The Petrine office and its mission must be defined in terms of the church instead of the church being defined in terms of the papacy.

Second, there is the task of reaching an agreement on the commission given to Peter in the Bible and on its significance for an ecumenical community of churches at the present time and in

the future. To this end, we must acknowledge the developments
and changes of form which the Petrine office has undergone in
the course of many centuries. Of special interest should be the
understanding, form, and practice of the Petrine office in the first
centuries when the church was still undivided and understood itself to be an ecumenical community of churches. Even though
there can be no return to the early church, we can certainly learn
from it. Knowledge of the historical changes in the form of the
Petrine office gives us the freedom to shape this office according
to the unique needs of the present and the future. If this second
task is to be successful, there must also be agreement on a common method of interpreting the scriptures, tradition and history,
and the signs of the times.

Third, on the basis of an ecclesiology of communion, the
Catholic Church, with the help of the other churches, must renew and develop, more consistently than hitherto, its own form
as a communion of churches. Only if the church takes the form
of a communion will the Petrine office take a communal form.

In all three of these tasks we do not start at point zero today.
In the area of theology many studies and proposals have already
been published that lead us farther along the way. Vatican II and
postconciliar reforms have taken the first steps. In the ecumenical realm, the dialogue between Lutherans and Catholics in the
United States on the church and the Petrine office has thus far
been among the most productive.[16]

In conclusion, let me offer, in regard to the third task, concerning church structures, some comments that emerge from current
observations.

Frequently we come up against the view that communion has
nothing to do with juridical or organizational structures — that
it describes only a way of thinking, the spirit of communion, and
corresponding personal behavior. It is true, of course, that forms
of participation are, in fact, empty, dead structures if they are not

---

16. See Paul C. Empie and T. Austin Murphy, eds., *Papal Primacy and the Universal Church* (Minneapolis: Augsburg, 1974); "Teaching Authority and Infallibility
in the Church," in *Theological Studies* 39 (1979): 113–66.

animated by the spirit of communion. On the other hand, like all of life, a living communion cannot develop if it is not given scope, forms, and structures.

It is an illusion to think that communion means total harmony. The people who think this way believe they can appeal to a good many formulations of Vatican II, in which communion is presented as an ideal and is described as a gift of the Holy Spirit. However, the language of the council is meant to be taken as normative and not simply idealistic; when the council speaks of trusting in the Holy Spirit, it does not by any means intend to exclude structures of communion. Nevertheless, those who are critical or call for structures of participation are often accused of disturbing harmony and being mistrustful of the action of the Holy Spirit. However, accusations of this sort confuse communion with harmony.

The recommendation of the *spirit* of communion instead of *structures* of participation, and the confusion of *communion* with total *harmony* are sometimes used to support persisting monopolies of responsibilities and powers, as well as centralization. Communion is here interpreted as the duty to practice a subordination that is called for in the name of the spirit of communion.

Structures of communion are also needed so conflicts, which are unavoidable in a living church, may not be suppressed but can be dealt with and resolved in a Christian and orderly way. The central conflict that determined the course of the debates at Vatican I and II may serve as an example. It was the conflict between the paradigms of the church in the first and second millennia. Each one of the paradigms represented a basic function of the church; the conflict between them expressed a vital process of deepening awareness and growth. The communion of witnesses to a tradition that must be preserved (the first millennium paradigm) had to became a communion of all those who actively shape this tradition in order to keep it alive (the second millennium paradigm). However, for the time being that vital process of deepening awareness has achieved only a partial expression. In the course of the second millennium, a monopoly on decision-making turned the pope increasingly into the sole agent in the active shaping of the church and tradition.

The conflict at Vatican I and II arose because the bishops, as official witnesses to the tradition, were now also demanding to participate in the active shaping of the church and tradition; they were, therefore, calling for structures of collegial participation. Another expression of deepening consciousness and growth is the conflict now going on, after Vatican II, under the false and misleading name of a "democratization" of the church. Appealing to the teaching of the council on the people of God, active believers are demanding, as laypersons, to be included in the shaping of the church's life. However, structures of communion and participation are not only the object of demands; these participatory structures also make it possible to resolve the conflicts.

The development of structures of communion needs to be guided by three principles. The first is the principle of *catholicity:* These structures must make it possible for a multiplicity of agents and the many-sidedness of life to find space in the church to replace existing centralization and uniformity. The second is the principle of *collegiality* and *cooperation:* These structures must make it possible for decision-making to take a collegial form and for the determination of decisions to be made to involve the co-operation of all the faithful. The third is the principle of *subsidiarity:* These structures must make it possible for decisions that do not threaten the unity and communion of the universal church to be made within limited regions of the church. The application of these three principles does not weaken the papacy; on the contrary, it presupposes a center of unity and a ministry of communion acknowledged by all.

The full application of the three principles of catholicity, collegiality, and subsidiarity is not possible, however, without the restoration of the original three-membered, or triadic, form of church structure. In the early church this form was the most important principle at work in the organization of the universal church: the particular church with its bishop; the regional ecclesiastical units, especially the patriarchal churches with their patriarchs; and for the universal church, the pope. In a passage of

Vatican II that was cited earlier (LG 23), the development of the intermediate level is ascribed to divine providence; on this issue, the council gives first place to "the ancient patriarchal churches."

Vatican II gave us a very specific description of the function of these regional structures of communion. Such structures make it possible for the particular churches, "while safeguarding the unity of faith..., to have their own discipline, enjoy their own liturgical usage and inherit a theological and spiritual patrimony." They also allow the churches of a region to be linked among themselves "by bonds of a more intimate charity in what pertains to the sacramental life and in a mutual respect for rights and obligations" (LG 23). In fact, in the early church these regional structures had a twofold function.[17] They made it possible for the churches of a region to enjoy a more concrete and closer kind of communication and communion than is possible over the expanse of the universal church; and in their common faith, and through the patriarchal church, they were linked to the universal church. Furthermore, the regional structures made it possible for these churches to acquire a distinctive form that was independent, yet rooted in the surrounding cultural world; together with the other churches of the same region, they could preserve and develop this distinctive form. In other words, they made inculturation possible.

The patriarchal churches were governed by the patriarchs, together with the synod of bishops. In the first millennium the papacy recognized their administrative autonomy and special heritages. It intervened only rarely, especially in important questions of faith, and then only when it was called upon as a court of appeal. In the West there was the Latin patriarchate of the bishop of Rome. Only when the patriarchal structure of the West came to be understood as the structure for the universal church did the two-membered, or dual, structural form replace the triadic. Only then did the church of the West lose its character as a communion of churches and replace this with uniformity and

---

17. See Gisbert Greshake, "Zwischeninstanzen zwischen Papst und Ortsbischöfen," in Hubert Müller and Hermann J. Pottmeyer, eds., *Die Bischofskonferenz: Theologischer und juridischer Status* (Düsseldorf: Patmos, 1989), 97–106.

centralization. On the other hand, the Eastern church, now lacking the center of unity and the ministry of communion, saw its unity disintegrate into a multiplicity of autocephalous or autonomous churches, which have not found their way to a workable communion among themselves.

The renewal and further development of the triadic form of church structure is, then, an essential condition for the church to regain its original distinctive form as a communion of churches. Only within this triadic form can the collegiality of the episcopate and the participation of the entire people of God become active forces without having their claims lead immediately and inevitably to a polarization between pope, episcopate, and local churches. Joseph Ratzinger was, therefore, one of the first to call, even during the council, for the "building up of patriarchal spaces" in which "the consciousness of reciprocal interconnections at the horizontal level" can develop.[18] The establishment of continental episcopal conferences and the holding of continental synods can be first steps in this direction.

Closely connected with this proposal is another that refers to the pope and results from the renewal of the triadic division: the separation of the Petrine and the patriarchal functions of the bishop of Rome. Soon after the council, Ratzinger described this as a "task for the future: to separate more clearly the office proper to the successor of Peter from the patriarchal office and, where necessary, to create new patriarchates and separate them from the Latin church." For "a uniform canon law, a uniform liturgy, a uniform filling of episcopal sees by the Roman central administration — all of these are things that do not necessarily accompany the primacy as such, but result only from this close union of two offices."[19] The primacy by its nature, according to Ratzinger, "does not necessarily entail the position of Rome as an administrative center (centralization), but entails only the spiritual and juridical power that goes with responsibility for the

---

18. Ratzinger, "Konkrete Formen," 159, 161.
19. Ratzinger, *Das neue Volk Gottes*, 142.

word and for communion."[20] This distinctive form of the papal office in which the functions of the patriarch of the West have become a part of the apostolic primacy was described by Ratzinger as a "universal patriarchate."[21]

The separation of the patriarchal and Petrine functions of the pope must be matched by a breaking-up of the functions of the Roman Curia. Since the patriarchal responsibilities of the pope are a matter of ecclesiastical and not divine law, the corresponding functions of the Curia, says Ratzinger, can "definitely be shared by the episcopate throughout the world — in fact, the situation of the church undoubtedly demands such a sharing."[22] In this respect, "the college of bishops as such, together with the pope, could regard itself as superior to Curia and could cooperate in shaping it."[23] It is obvious that these suggestions are extremely important not only for the reform of the church and for the form of the Petrine office, but also for a truly ecumenical future.

For this reason the ecumenical Community of Dombes (Groupe des Dombes) took these proposals into its document on the ministry of communion within the universal church.[24] In the context of their own suggestions for a conversion of the confessions, the group sees it as the task of the Catholic Church to establish a balance between the communal, collegial, and personal dimensions of the Petrine ministry of communion.

In his remarkable book *The Office of Peter and the Structure of the Church,* Hans Urs von Balthasar likewise gives prominence to the perspectives provided by Vatican II for a papacy in communion. His starting point is the *Realsymbolik* of the biblical Peter, who was a "Peter within the structure" of the different vocations of Mary and the other apostles. It was part of

---

20. Joseph Ratzinger, "Primat," in *Lexikon für Theologie und Kirche* (Freiburg: Herder, 1963), 8:763.

21. Ratzinger, "Konkrete Formen," 157.

22. Joseph Ratzinger, "Ekklesiologische Bemerkungen zum Schema 'De Episcopis,'" in *do-c* no. 135 (1964), 5.

23. Ratzinger, "Konkrete Formen," 158.

24. Groupe des Dombes, *Le ministère de communion dans l'Église universelle* (Paris: Centurion, 1986), 89–98.

Peter's commission to set the others free for service in their special mission.

> Vatican II, incorporating the achievements of Vatican I, endeavors to express more articulately and more fully the unique correlation of Church unity in *communio,* collegiality and primacy.... While it is necessary to justify the eccentricity of the Petrine office, it can only be done without danger if this office manifests its function [of effectively embodying unity] in practice at the heart of the *communio* and the *collegium,* making for liberation through integration. This now has a good chance to succeed, as the last two Councils have directed the whole *communio* of the Church, as well as the entire college of bishops, to allow the Petrine office space in which to exercise its function. If both things take place in the spirit of mutual eucharistic *communio,* the pilgrim Church will be able to be an anticipatory reflection of the perfect Church, without overplaying her role...as pilgrim and penitent.[25]

"To set the others free for service in their special mission": that is precisely the service to be rendered by the structures of communion; this is the perspective of Vatican II. Consequently, the renewal and further development of these structures does not signify a limitation or weakening of the Petrine office; rather it is an essential part of the Petrine commission. The more the universal church becomes once again a communion of churches, the more clearly the structures of communion recover their distinctive form, and the more the church gains in catholicity: the more the church will need the Petrine ministry of communion and be able to understand this Petrine ministry as a gift of God to the church.

---

25. Hans Urs von Balthasar, *The Office of Peter and the Structure of the Church* (San Francisco: Ignatius Press, 1986), 220f.; see Hermann J. Pottmeyer, "Why Does the Church Need a Pope?" *Communio* 18 (1991): 304–12.

Index